The Great War Illustrated

The
Home Front

Final Blows and the Year of Victory

David Bilton

D1337574

Pen & Sword
MILITARY

First published in Great Britain in 2018 by
Pen & Sword Military
An imprint of
Pen & Sword Books Ltd
47 Church Street
Barnsley
South Yorkshire
S70 2AS

Copyright © David Bilton 2018

ISBN 978 1 47383 368 5

Typeset by Aura Technology and Software Services, India
Printed and bound in England by CPI Group (UK) Ltd, Croydon, CR0 4YY

Pen & Sword Books Limited incorporates the imprints of Atlas, Archaeology,
Aviation, Discovery, Family History, Fiction, History, Maritime, Military,
Military Classics, Politics, Select, Transport, True Crime, Air World, Frontline
Publishing, Leo Cooper, Remember When, Seaforth Publishing, The Praetorian
Press, Wharncliffe Local History, Wharncliffe Transport, Wharncliffe True Crime
and White Owl.

For a complete list of Pen & Sword titles please contact
PEN & SWORD BOOKS LIMITED
47 Church Street, Barnsley, South Yorkshire, S70 2AS, England
E-mail: enquiries@pen-and-sword.co.uk
Website: www.pen-and-sword.co.uk

Contents

Acknowledgements

As with previous books, a great big thank you to the staff of the Prince Consort's Library and Reading Central Library for their help, kindness and knowledge during the pre-writing stages of this book. Once again, many thanks to my friend Anne Coulson for checking, correcting and suggesting. While some of the pictures come from books mentioned in the bibliography, some are from my own collection.

Introduction

This book is the fifth volume in a series that illustrates life on the Home Front during each year of the war. The many photographs show life through the eyes of those not on the military frontline. The book portrays the life of ordinary citizens and how they experienced the war. Important people appear only as part of the context of everyday life.

This book is not solely about Britain; though the major part of it does record British life, I have attempted to show the international commonality of various themes through illustrations from other Allied and enemy countries. Readers may be familiar with some, but most have not been published since the war, and others have never been published. As the photographs form the main focus of the book, I have quoted liberally from my previous books on the Home Front to provide the historical context, using the experiences of Hull and Reading as often typical but sometimes contrasting examples.

This is a book about the Home Front on an international scale. It is not chronological; it is themed, though topics do cross over. Similarly, the difference between being in the forces and being on the Home Front is a grey area. It took a long time to train new recruits, and that training was done on the Home Front. In many areas, there were more people in uniform than out of it, a fact that became accepted as part of life.

What was 'The Home Front'? There are many interpretations of the phrase: 'the sphere of civilian activity in war'; 'the civilian sector of a nation at war when its armed forces are in combat abroad'; 'the name given to the part of war that was not actively involved in the fighting but which was vital to it'; an 'informal term for the civilian populace of the nation at war as an active support system of the military who depend on Home Front civilian support services such as factories that build materiel to support the military front'. More simply it refers to 'life in Britain during the war itself'. All of these have elements of truth but none fully describe the range of experiences that shaped the Home Front.

If this book is about life away from the combat zone, then some of what happened on the Home Front cannot be recorded here. For those caught in a Zeppelin raid, the Home Front became a war zone; it was not always 'All quiet on the Home Front' as assumed by the title of one oral history book. In this, and previous volumes, I have defined the Home Front as the totality of the experience of the civilian population in a country affected, directly or indirectly, by the war. As there were considerable numbers of military personnel on the Home Front, interacting with the civilian population, they too are included.

This again needs some examination. The Home Front was not a singular experience. Life in the countryside was different to that in the town or city, the latter being more quickly affected by change. However, life in the Scottish Isles differed from life in the Kent countryside. Again, life in a coastal town on the east of the country was unlike that on the west. Of course the whole country experienced basic similarities but there were many factors that varied the war's effects. How could a family who lost their only son experience the same war as a neighbour with five serving sons who all returned? What similarities were there between the family of a conscientious objector and one whose father/husband had been killed, or between an Irish family and a Welsh one?

While there is a common link between all of these examples, what links can be found between Belgian, French, Dutch, German, Japanese or Russian families? All these countries had a Home Front and all were directly affected by the war. There are some obvious differences. Neutral Holland was quickly affected by the war on its borders, and Japan, an isolated Allied Power, fought in the Pacific and escorted convoys to Europe but was otherwise largely unaffected. Both were unlike the other countries which, despite some differences, were all united by an invasion, long or short, of their Home Fronts.

We can add further layers to the civilian experience of the war through the Home Front. Neutral countries had to defend themselves against possible aggression and were on a war footing which inevitably affected civilian life. They were not at war, so nationals of the warring countries were free to move about as before the war and spying was rife. As safe havens, they became the guardians of hundreds of refugees or prisoners of war. And, as in the warring countries, commodities became short because, once at sea, their ships became targets.

Combatant countries on the continent experienced two types of Home Front, the obvious one being the civilians behind the fighting front. But in an occupied country civilians were behind both sides of the line. All shared the same nationality, but lived on the Home Front, very differently, enduring different constraints.

The topic of the Home Front for just one year across only the combatant nations would require considerably more space than is available in a book of this size. As this is essentially an illustrated book it cannot cover any topic to a great depth; the text is secondary, the pictures tell the story. This book therefore illustrates life on the Home Front for civilians on both sides of the wire.

TO ALL AT HOME.

GWI-HF_1 In the 2 January edition of *Punch* the message was clear.

CARRYING ON !

We are inclined to take pride in our record for the four years of War.

2,500 of our trained men have left us to join the Forces.

We have had to fill their places with women who were, of necessity, inexperienced in the trade.

We have had to undertake a huge increase of work to carry out the various rationing schemes.

We have met our difficulties as they arose with the minimum of disadvantage to our customers.

If new ones arise, we shall still hope to overcome them and to

CARRY ON.

International Stores

THE BIGGEST GROCERS IN THE WORLD

TEA :: COFFEE :: GROCERIES :: PROVISIONS

I.S. 122

GWI-HF_2 International Stores was the biggest grocery chain in Britain and was proud of its contribution to the war effort.

PEACE SHALL FLOURISH!
(Planting the Olive Tree)

Viel Glück im neuen Jahre

GWI-HF_3 The wish for peace was international. A British card suggesting it was time to plant the peace and let it flourish.

GWI-HF_5 A recycled card: paper was in very short supply. It was sold on behalf of the German Red Cross to raise funds to help the wounded. In the top left is the monument to the Battle of the Nations that commemorates Napoleon's defeat at Leipzig in 1813.

GWI-HF_4 A German New Year card wishing the recipient much luck in the coming year. The pigs are wishful thinking as meat was only available in very small quantities and was strictly rationed.

Erinnerung
an die Kriegsjahre
1914|18.

The Home Fronts in 1918

Stick it!

'As 1917 turned into 1918, the problems remained the same and would do so for some time. There were shortages of food and men for the army, prices were rising, and there was industrial unrest and air raids to deal and contend with. Apart from final victory there was to be one other high point of the coming year, the granting of the vote to many women.'

In the forty-nine months since the war had started, much had changed. Around the world everyone fervently hoped the war would end but no one was really prepared for such a dramatic change as the end of the greatest war ever fought. While the Allies were preparing for victory in 1919, the Germans were preparing for the war to end in 1918, now Russia was no longer an issue; but 'there's many a slip 'twixt cup and lip' – a thought indicated in June when Ludendorff said that the war could last longer than planned.

For Germany, prospects were dark unless a quick victory was achieved. Economic life was threatened with paralysis through lack of coal, oils and lubricants and the breakdown of the railways. The Allies could rely on vast manpower reinforcements from America while Germany's manpower resources were virtually exhausted.

While the combatants readied themselves for yet another year of war, and the Home Fronts got ready to tighten their belts even further, the arrival of large numbers of American troops was set to change the outcome. President Wilson, even though a newcomer to the war, addressed Congress in January with his fourteen points for peace, adding a further five points in September.

The *Reading Chronicle* introduced the New Year with serious words: 'Whether 1918 will end the war may be uncertain. That it will decide the issue is clear. It will be a year of trial, endurance and sacrifice, in which every citizen is called upon to lend a hand.' Reverend Canon Fowler of Earley wrote in the Parish magazine of his disappointment that peace had not been secured but that he was sure God would grant it in his own good time. The Archbishop of Canterbury, preaching at Westminster Abbey, told the congregation, 'We persist and must persist in our task.' Churchill was of the same opinion, telling Lord Riddell prophetically, 'We must fight to a finish… you never know when the Germans will crash.'

Two hundred miles north, the people of Hull were told that the war would be 'won by the nation, or group of nations, whose civilian population can endure the most heroically, and can control itself the longest.' The *Eastern Morning News* noted there was no hopeful sign that the bloodshed and destruction was at the point of coming to an end but regardless of the grim outlook, it still wished its readers 'A Happy New Year'.

'In Britain the bleak New Year of 1918 opened with a day of national prayer.' The Sunday services were crowded.

There was not much good news. Barely a week into the month came news of a naval loss: HMS *Racoon* struck rocks at the Garvan Isles, sinking with the loss of all her crew.

For many there was a feeling that the war would go on forever. Lloyd George recalled the 'bewilderment and hardships of the time, war tiredness, the ghastly losses, the receding horizon of victory'. With non-essential work like painting having been stopped earlier in the war, most towns and cities were now drab, shabby and colourless. Even the people were shabby and the colour of their clothes matched the drabness of their lives and the towns they lived in. 'Well-worn shabbiness' became the accepted thing.

In Germany, everything was now aimed at maximising munitions output and a speedy end to the war. An example was the message of the commander of the Berlin garrison. He told strikers that their choice was to return to work or be shot.

Germany began to feel the effects of industrial unrest at the start of the year with random acts of sabotage in January. These were followed by strikes in Berlin, Essen, Hamburg, Leipzig and elsewhere, affecting all aspects of the war effort. In Berlin a strike by 250,000 threatened the preparations for the March offensive. In some areas there was rioting accompanied by violence. Strikes now had a revolutionary aspect with workers demanding rights, a shock to the government and army. The July strikes in the Silesian coal mines were simply about food. The miners were insufficiently fed to work the hours demanded and therefore wanted a cut in hours. Even with the military proclaiming a state of siege, the unrest continued into August.

Lengthening casualty lists in Britain meant further combing-out of those in previously starred (reserved) employment. Naturally this was followed by the increased employment of women and, by 1918, processes had been set in place that allowed the mass mobilisation of women, not just on the Home Front but in the armed forces where they released men to serve at the front. They were also needed on the land. Campaigns throughout spring and early summer aimed to recruit more women to the land and into hospitals. Their reward would be the vote, albeit only after the age of 30, but women could become MPs at the age of 21.

The manpower shortage for the army could only be solved by increasing call-up of previously exempt groups and ages, regardless of the effect on production of coal and munitions. The Manpower Bill put forward by Lloyd George combed out munition workers up to age 50, but those aged over 40 were liable only to Home Service. This resulted in over 100,000 munitions workers and 50,000 pit workers being released for the army. Later this was followed by a lowering of the minimum age of call-up to 17½ and in May all 19 and 20-year-olds were called up. A month later this was extended to include all those born between 1895 and 1897 except workers in shipbuilding and at oil shale works. This extension of conscription caused great difficulties to many families, resulting in many applications for exemption. It also hit key people in science, industry and business. In order to counter any invasion, it was proposed to form a militia of every male up to the age of 60. A further proposal to conscript both the Irish and the Clergy was reversed before it went through Parliament.

Much of this was a result of the fact that in south coast towns, and even as far inland as Wimbledon, the rumble of the guns could be heard. There was no opposition either from previously staunch defenders of their workers. Realising the severity of the situation, the unions offered no resistance.

Germany and France tackled the increasing shortage of men for the army by calling up the 1920 class.

The importance of numbers was shown by Lloyd George who stated, 'the last man may count.' On 5 August he sent a simple and very plain message to the Empire: 'Hold Fast'.

Men in reserved occupations at 31/10/18 (from National Service registers)

Year of birth	Railway & transport	Coalminers	Agricultural	Munitions, shipbuilding & ship repairs	Other certified occupations	Total
1900	18,824	36,498	22,849	29,850	15,157	123,178
1895 to 1899	42,929	67,885	36,554	91,044	6,943	245,355
1890 to 1894	55,610	79,261	42,148	173,079	19,232	369,330
1885 to 1889	78,096	96,588	63,289	225,900	44,284	508,157
1876 to 1884	168,462	179,836	137,7333	444,379	147,391	1,077,801
1874 to 1875	37,720	42,641	37,933	67,929	64,816	251,039
Grand total	401,641	502,709	340,506	1,032,181	297,823	2,574,860

Not every government department felt the same. In February, just weeks before the German offensive to end the war, the British Labour Ministry announced demobilisation arrangements. And a few weeks later, Churchill in a War Cabinet memo asked, 'How are we going to win the war in 1919?' Six months later his question was whether the war was to be won in 1919 or 1920.

The call-up was not universally respected. In Quebec there were riots about conscription which had started in 1917. The situation was so serious that troops were used to quell the disturbances and four were killed when they opened fire.

Conscription continued to be opposed in Britain with many absolutists serving prison sentences. Bertrand Russell was convicted and sentenced in the summer of 1918 for making statements likely to prejudice relations with America. His punishment was six months in the Second Division (to which many conscientious objectors were sentenced), but this was overturned by his friends pulling strings so he could serve his time in the comfort of the First Division: a relatively light sentence.

A different situation existed for those conscripted into the Austrian army, in which many no longer wanted to serve. It was estimated that by July there were 250,000 deserters; some roaming in groups armed with machine guns and some even possessing light artillery.

In Germany the comb-out was more ruthless. Anyone who could hold a rifle was drafted, aided by the closing of non-essential factories due to the shortage of materials. Young men vanished from the streets and even one-armed men were found tasks suitable to their ability. 'Germany was being bled white in a vast and final mustering of her manpower.'

With materials prioritised for war production, fewer and fewer essential goods were available. Limited production meant making the most out of what was available, but interestingly shops still managed to hold January sales. For most the major issue was the rising cost of living, even though wages were rising.

Table comparing prices of beef, bread, butter and milk (percentage change) between 1914 and 1918.

Country	July 1914	July 1917	July 1918
United Kingdom	100	185	179
France	100	170	203
Italy	100	149	256
United States	100	140	153
Sweden	100	160	268
Switzerland	100	180	213
Germany	100	181	249
Austria	100	318	302

As in 1917, food was a continuing problem although food supplies were now better – the 1917 harvest had been a record one. There were still lengthy queues and much resentment about the ways in which the wealthy always got their share, so much that full delivery baskets leaving a shop's backdoor were sometimes looted. As the poor struggled to obtain sufficient basic necessities their children began to show signs of malnutrition: in Germany they were reported to be 'thin and pale as corpses…mere skin and bone'. Such were the shortages that even the better-off had taken to asking dinner guests to bring some food with them.

The government had no choice but to introduce rationing, initially in London and the Home Counties, slowly extending it to the rest of the country. Before this the government had told the population to 'Eat slowly. You will need less food' and to 'Keep warm. You will need less food.' How they were supposed to keep warm during a coal shortage was not explained.

Like Britain, French newspapers provided ingenious recipes, using easily available ingredients, to help replace the shortage of staples such as pasta, and reiterated the importance of economy. And, again like Britain, appeals asked shoppers to use margarine instead of butter, substitute saccharin for sugar and replace fresh milk with condensed. Schoolchildren designed posters to reduce consumption: 'Don't waste bread'; 'Economise bread by eating potatoes'; 'Eat fish to save our livestock'. As in most of the warring countries, nobody believed that war bread was better than that sold pre-war.

The first commodity to be rationed was sugar. 'Robert Graves, married in January, had to save a month's sugar, along with butter, for his three-tiered wedding cake. Even then the cake had a plaster case of imitation icing.' Another indication of the shortage of food was the Mansion House luncheon to celebrate the first anniversary of the American entry into the war: 'No meat was served, and the fare – soup, fish, eggs, vegetables and fruit – was said to be the plainest ever offered.' This contrasted with the laxity shown in France where 'a Paris publisher entertained guests to a luncheon consisting of Goose sausage, Woodcock, flambées à la fine champagne, Baron de Pauillac [beef] à la purée de champignons, truffles en croute, Langoustes en Bellevue, Salade Russe, Mont-Blanc [dessert], and three choice wines.' This was after legislation to curb superfluous consumption!

In Germany, in January, the renowned Adlon Hotel in Berlin provided, as a typical meal, 'one sardine, three thin slices of smoked salmon, soup that was little more than hot salty water, two small boiled potatoes and a substitute for "corn-starch" pudding. There was no butter or sauces.' Salt was scarce and wine was new and vinegary. 'Menus were innocent of fish, eggs and vegetables.' As a result of the shortages, restaurants in Berlin began to close, as did many shops.

The meal at the Adlon was a feast compared to what was generally offered: 'potatoes and swedes, accompanied by various tasteless substitute dishes'. Goulash became a mystery meal of unidentified ingredients. The sausage was an alternative. In Victorian England sausages were known as 'little parcels of wonder' – the buyer wondered what was in them. In Britain, meat control and inspection meant that the purchaser knew what they were buying during the war; it was not so in Germany where sausages contained mostly swede with the addition of offal, horse-flesh and even dog. Meat was so short in May the kangaroos in Berlin Zoo were slaughtered for meat. However, in contrast to the sufferings of their subjects, the Prince and Princess Blücher gave a reception for 150 distinguished guests. 'It was a brilliant affair, resplendent with jewels and multi-coloured uniforms, and the company was regaled with the richest foods from the Blücher country estate.' Although it was generally known that the population was suffering, the Spanish Ambassador regretted the absence of the British Prime Minister, because, he opined, this would show him how nonsensical it was to think that Germany was starving.

Sugar rationing in Britain was followed in April by meat and bacon via the meat card, and also the food card for butter, lard and margarine. Over 40 million of each of these types of card were issued. After registering with a butcher and a grocer, each individual's ration of 16 ounces of meat, 5 ounces of bacon and 4 ounces of margarine or butter every week was guaranteed. Children under the age of six got half the meat ration of an adult, while adolescents and heavy workers received extra allowances.

One positive to this was inspection. The potential dilution of sundries such as sausages and pies was solved by inspectors checking the content. On a humorous note, it was suggested that vegetarian boarders should be encouraged as their meat coupons could be traded for bags of nuts which were not rationed. Being a vegetarian in Britain was an option which Germans did not have: there were few nuts and vegetables available.

With fair distribution of these basic commodities queues disappeared; previously every Saturday in London the police had estimated 500,000 were standing in queues for food. Shopping now became agreeable to requirements and purse.

In France, meatless days increased during the year to three a week, but generally fewer goods were rationed. Queues were common except for rationed goods, where everyone knew waiting in line made no difference to what they would get.

In July, ration books replaced the ration cards. As food was essential it should have been a simple job to give out the ration books to everyone, but this was not the case. Taking Hull as a typical city, we see that although the council sent out 227,000 books, this did not cover everyone. Some 25,000 people forgot to apply or simply forgot to put their address.

The food was there; the only problem was the price which was not affected by rationing. Compared to the Central Powers, Britain was comparatively well off. Throughout the war most things were still available and were never rationed, while in Germany and Austria every foodstuff was rationed with some becoming unobtainable.

Comparison of food rationing

Foodstuff	Britain*	Germany **	Austria **
Bread	Not rationed#	3lbs 13¼ ounces	2lbs 2 ounces
Meat	16 ounces	7 ounces	4.6 ounces
Fish	Not rationed	0.87 ounces	Not obtainable
Milk	Not rationed	1½ pints	0.58 pints
Eggs	Not rationed	0.25 of an egg	Not obtainable
Butter	4 ounces	1.05 ounces	1 ounce
Sugar	8 ounces	8 ounces	3½ ounces
Cereals	Not rationed	2.19 ounces	1.4 ounces
Cheese	Not rationed	1.09 ounces	¾ ounce
Jam	Not rationed	3½ ounces	2.4 ounces
Syrup	Not rationed	0.87 ounces	0.58 ounces
Fruit	Not rationed	Not obtainable	11.7 ounces
Tea	Not rationed	Ersatz – 1.75 ounces	Ersatz – 1.1 ounces
Coffee	Not rationed	Ersatz – 2.19 ounces	Ersatz – 1.4 ounces
Cocoa	Not rationed	Not obtainable	Not obtainable
Potatoes	Not rationed	6 lbs	7 lbs
Vegetables	Not rationed	5 to 10 lbs	2 lbs 12 ounces

*Not rationed but some commodities like milk were restricted or locally rationed until towards the end of the war when rationing for some goods was in effect.
By the end of the war a working man received 1lb per day and a working woman 4lb a week.
**Weekly allowance

Britain was fortunate that the bread supply was adequate and did not need to be rationed. France, which was a major wheat producer, was forced to introduce a daily ration of 10 ounces per head in January, less than Britain which imported a large amount of wheat. The shortage was not in France but in Italy which had to be supplemented by French grain. This reduction to less than half the normal amount consumed led to brawls in bakeries and queues to lay in bread before the rationing date. The reduction meant that a meal in a restaurant with bread, limited to one roll, required coupons. It also led to a ban on luxury pastries.

Weekly per head consumption of essential foodstuffs in an average working class family in Britain

Foodstuff	Lbs 1914	Lbs 1918	% change
Bread and flour	7.33	7.55	+3
Meat	1.49	0.96	-36
Bacon	0.26	0.56	+115
Lard	0.22	0.17	-23
Butter	0.37	0.17	-54
Margarine	0.09	0.20	+122
Potatoes	3.41	4.38	+28
Cheese	0.18	0.09	-50
Sugar	1.29	0.62	-52

Possibly the greatest hardship for many was the shortage of tea. When it was found that a shop had received supplies a queue quickly formed, often necessitating police control. The other essential for many was tobacco which in Britain was available throughout the war but not always in the quantities desired. In Germany it was almost unobtainable.

The paper to wrap goods in was also in short supply, with newspapers (although they had been cut in size) having first call on any supplies. Collecting waste paper was now big business. In April 3,000 tons were collected in Britain.

Paper was among the everyday commodities which were almost unavailable in Germany. 'Chemists were almost without drugs, music shops had no strings for musical instruments and corset manufacture ceased through lack of suitable materials.' And although newspapers carried adverts for cameras, there was no photographic paper available. Rarely at the top of anyone's favourite places to visit, the dentist could now be avoided because there was almost no gold available for fillings.

Overseas supply meant that in Britain, given the ship was not sunk by U-boat attack, essentials like leather and cotton were available but controlled. The government took over footwear production to ensure that 'government shoes/boots' were available. Although the army had first call on wool supplies, it was still available, along with cotton from the empire; Britain was comparatively well clothed. In Germany the blockade reduced cotton supplies to those from Turkey and leather to the area controlled by German forces so that by mid-1918 'the footwear and clothing situation was becoming disastrous'. Instead of shoes many now wore 'wooden-soled clogs or sandals with cloth uppers'. It was possible, but difficult, for those with money to get what they wanted. A passable leather shoe was obtainable for a bribe of a pound of butter or a few bottles of wine, payment of 150 marks and a six-month wait. Cheaper shoes were available but they did not last long.

Clothing in Germany was so scarce that men were ordered to surrender any suits they had above the permitted two. Mending became difficult with queues for the small amount of thread available. What reasonable quality clothing there was, cost up to ten times the normal price.

In Britain, rising costs had led to demands for higher wages. The increase in the cost of basic foodstuffs was calculated throughout the war – the RFP index. Most months it moved up but occasionally it fell. Starting in August 1914 with a rise of 15 per cent, by August it had reached 118 per cent and by the end of war stood at 129 percent. Although food costs had more than doubled by the end of the war, they were higher in France and Italy. In neutral Sweden and Switzerland they were 268 and 213 per cent respectively. In Germany it stood at 249 per cent and in Austria 302 per cent.

As was already common in Germany, local authorities in Britain assisted the population in receiving adequate food provided by the national kitchens. They quickly spread from their point of origin in the poorer parts of London, and by August there were 623 of them spread across the country (not always in the poorer areas). They were not restaurants (although some did have dining facilities). Most of the meals purchased were taken from the premises to eat at home. Their cheapness came from an ability to buy in bulk and large-scale preparation. They could produce meals that were far more appetising than a wage-earner's household could easily manage. Such meals were purchased in exchange for the ration coupons issued to each member of a family. A typical range of food offered by a national kitchen included oxtail soup, Irish stew, potatoes, beans, bread, jam roll and rice pudding. Using such facilities also helped reduce the effects of shortages as there was less wastage and correct sized portions could be prepared and sold.

Another way to reduce shortages was the allotment: by 1918 they were on any available space. They were so popular that some areas ran out of land. To cope with this, parkland was dug up for the duration of the war. Kew Gardens had 200 acres under cultivation and even the flowerbeds around the Queen Victoria Memorial outside Buckingham Palace were planted with vegetables in April. While Britain never really suffered from a shortage of vegetables, the severe frost in France led to a scarcity of cabbages, carrots, cauliflower and swede: they were obtainable only for a high price. Like food and meals in restaurants, money ensured there was no shortage. In France the rules and restrictions were never as stringent as in Britain.

One way in which allotments could help was in combating shortages of the potato. Production was well short of demand. A typical example was the county of York which produced 297,000 tons but consumed 397,000 tons, a shortfall of 90,700 tons. To combat the shortage Lord Rhondda and Mr Prothero MP, an agricultural expert, appealed to every man who had a farm, a garden or an allotment to plant more potatoes to make the county self-supporting.

Food hoarding was a crime and one man was fined £500 and sentenced to a month's imprisonment for his private stock of food: 144lbs of sugar, 14 hams, 37 tins of sardines plus other things. While food shortages led some people to hoard, they encouraged others to try different foods, like horseflesh at 1/- a pound.

Once again, those with money could always find what they wanted: the black market thrived wherever there was a shortage. In Germany food controls were circumvented by literally going underground: animals were kept and fattened in cellars before being illegally sold.

Although the warring nations bombed civilian targets, overall the risk was comparatively low and the gap between the 'frontkampfers' and the rest of the population continued to grow. The former rarely talked about their experiences with the latter because there were no words to explain their reality: 'I'd like to see a tank come down the stalls' seemed to express how many soldiers felt about civilian life.

In Britain, outside London, towns and cities had to devise ways to deal with the shortage of meat. Throughout the previous year the position had worsened and only days into the New Year there was a dramatic reduction in availability. Hull, for example, suddenly found that only 20 per cent of its weekly requirement arrived. As there was little to sell, shops decided not to open for business on Mondays and Tuesdays. Alternatives such as eggs were suggested, along with low cost fish such as herrings and sprats. Game was also available, but at a price, and, when the government fixed the price of a rabbit at 2s 9d when the actual cost was 4s 9d, the supply dried up. In France it was the same: when the government fixed the price of potatoes they disappeared from the shops for two weeks. There the cost of game was less than 1917. Regardless how hard it was to obtain food in Britain, it was far harder in Germany and Austria.

Unnoticed on the Allied Home Front the blockade of Germany was bringing the German Home Front to its knees. Germany was 'near starvation and reduced to a miserable existence of ersatz makeshifts for clothing' and other goods. The German transport and industrial system was deteriorating through a lack of maintenance, renewal and repair; to such an extent that 'life was grinding to a halt', providing the conditions for revolt. Many were suffering from the cold weather because of a severe shortage of coal. As a result many simply went to bed very early in order to keep warm, and, as coal also provided lighting and everything closed early, there was little incentive to stay up.

The desire for food was added to that for peace. In February a report from Amsterdam told of 200,000 people marching in Charlottenburg crying, 'Peace! Bread!' A shot, followed by a police charge with sabres, resulted in the strikers manning barricades. From behind overturned trams they fired and hurled projectiles at the police. Many were wounded and numerous arrests were made.

The food situation in Germany was becoming desperate. 'For many Germans the main diet was very poor bread, swedes, and – when they were available – potatoes. Meat supplies were negligible. The all-embracing ration tickets were not available.' There was a severe shortage of fats in the diet that was evident by the 'yellowish, unhealthy pallor of the face'. Shortage of fats also meant limited soap production, affecting general health. Due to the fuel shortage, men had to shave in cold water, using an ersatz soap 'that irritated the skin and stopped up the drains'.

Eggs were only available on doctor's orders, and were virtually unobtainable. Even common vegetables like cabbages were hard to come by and expensive. Fruits like lemons and oranges were never available. Even the rich were not always able to satisfy their hunger.

The situation was not as severe in Britain but, as in Germany, coal was rationed. Gas and electricity supplies were reduced making homes colder and darker, there was a lack of hot water and cooking was difficult. Such was the shortage that 'it was a punishable offence to waste cinders, and newspapers published recipes for making briquettes with clay, coal-dust and tar as a cooking fuel.'

'The winter had brought rationing of gas, electricity and coal' to France as well. Most of the allowance went on cooking. Heating needs were met by wood when available: it was expensive, and there was a shortage of transport. Apartment dwellers in Paris who relied on central heating suffered when the landlord ran out of fuel. 'People were reduced to living in one room, with their overcoats on.' Naturally this affected social life and sitting around a friend's fire passed for an evening out as places of entertainment were closed four days a week to save fuel. Liquor sales were restricted, cafés and restaurants closed early and only two bus routes ran in Paris. The city was dead after 10 pm. It was worse in the provinces where candles provided light because of a shortage of paraffin.

The German transport system was in a dilapidated state. There were no buses in Berlin, just a few trams and any car seen was usually on official business. Trains were slow, overcrowded and liable to break down. The bicycle, essential as an alternative form of transport, also began to disappear due to a shortage of rubber. Coupled with food shortages normal life was breaking down.

In Britain ready-made meals from restaurants proved popular, as did meetings, provided the venue was heated. In order to save both heat and light many people spent long periods in bed. Restaurants were hit by the 'Curfew Order', whereby meals could not be cooked after 9.30 pm and lighting had to be extinguished thirty minutes later. The same order also meant that all places of entertainment had to end performances at 10.30 pm. The shortage of coal did not affect only householders: by September the furnaces on Teesside were also being affected.

Changes in fuel use 1914-18

Year	Coal (million tons used)	Oil (million gallons used)	Electricity (m Kwh)
1914	196	600	2,100
1918	207	1,350	4,000
Increase	3.5 %	125%	90%

The lack of fuel, coupled with rising costs, fewer railway seats and less track, further impacted civilian life. 'Whereas in previous years people had taken holidays, in 1918 they were classed as unpatriotic. There was no sport to occupy people's minds and there had been no return of the Bank Holidays taken away in the previous year. In general travel from home to work was proving difficult so anything as exotic as a holiday would probably have been impossible anyway. The train services continued to decline while fares rose by 50 per cent. In some areas there was no longer a service because the track was now serving its country in France. Petrol shortages worsened and the London rush hour became a nightmare: the new ministries had vastly increased the number of people who needed transport across London but at the same time the shortage of fuel meant less transport and overcrowding. "The scramble to get into some of the longer distance trains and omnibuses constituted a bear fight out of which those of both sexes who were worsted or driven off the over-laden vehicles... retreated to the pavement with hats bashed in, umbrellas broken, shins and ankles kicked and bruised, in a shaken condition." The general lack of petrol throughout the war meant that cycling, which had been losing ground before the war, due to the dust and danger of cars, regained its popularity.'

As in the previous year, women were taking over or working in more and more previously men-only occupations. By 1918 millions of women were in employment and as a reward for their contribution to the war effort, parliament had agreed in 1917 to women's suffrage.

Changes in Women's employment during the war

Type of employment	Number of Women	Employed	Percentage
	1914	1918	of 1914 total
Munitions	212,000	947,000	446
Textiles	863,000	818,000	95
Clothing	612,000	556,000	91
Other industries	452,000	451,000	99
Transport	18,000	117,000	650
Agriculture	190,000	228,000	120
Commerce	505,000	934,000	184
Self-employed	430,000	470,000	109
Hotels, Theatres	181,000	220,000	121.5
Professional	542,000	652,000	120
Domestic service	1,658,000	1,250,000	75
Local and national govern-ment (including teaching)	262,000	460,000	175
Totals	5,925,000	7,103,000	120%

'Similarly there was a need to reward the soldiers, sailors and airmen during the reconstruction for a better post-war world. The Representation of the People Act gave the vote to men over the age of 21 and women over the age of 30 provided they were householders or wives of householders or fulfilled certain other property qualifications. Although revolutionary, the act passed quietly into law during June 1918 giving 8.5 million women the vote and in November women over the age of 21 could stand as Members of Parliament (with one woman serving in 1918). What the act gave to many it also took away from a few; conscientious objectors were banned for five years after the war as a punishment for not fighting.'

Many hated the conscientious objectors but more hated the enemy. There had been riots earlier in the war but the alien problem had abated until the March offensive in France. The success of this 'offensive started a new wave of anti-German feeling. A 2 mile long petition, carrying over a million signatures, demanded the internment of all enemy aliens. Abuse was directed at both German people and German street names, many of which were changed as a result. Even the Royal Society expelled enemy aliens from its membership, and even as late as the end of September the crowds were demanding the removal of Sir Eyre Crowe from the Foreign Office because his mother was German and he had been educated in Europe (they ignored the fact that since 1885 he had followed a very unfriendly line towards Germany). While civilians were aware that the front was 'a place of horror', they were 'baffled by the soldiers' apparent refusal to hate "Old Fritz".'

'In the wake of this hatred for the enemy, conscientious objectors once again became the target of much public venom.' They became pariahs, sometimes to their own families, and as a result of their treatment and/or the abhorrence felt by authority some were classed as insane. Suspected pacifist activity was treated harshly. For having 100 copies of a proscribed peace pamphlet in his possession, a 71-year-old was imprisoned for six months.

Table showing increase in government expenditure to finance the war

War period	Amount in Pounds
1914-15 (eight months)	362,000,000
1915-16	1,420,000,000
1916-17	2,010,000,000
1917-18	2,450,000,000
1918 (April to August)	1,800,000,000
Total for four years	8,042,000,000

The average expenditure per day in 1914-15 was £1,500,000, a year later it was £3,750,000 and by 1917-18 it was £6,986,000. The extra money had to come from somewhere.

War was a costly business. The government had initially relied upon the vast wealth created during the Victorian era to pay for it. However, this was insufficient and to increase income 'consecutive war budgets had increased income tax, increased taxes on all sorts of goods and imposed a "super tax" on the wealthy.' In 1916 income tax had been raised from 3s. 6d. to 5s. on income over £2,500, not £3,000 as previously. In 1918 it was raised to 6s. and super-tax increased from 3s. 6d. to 4s. 6d. Stamp duty on cheques was doubled in 1918 and the minimum charge for a letter was increased to 1½d. and for postcards to 1d.

In the 1918 budget there was also a substantial increase in indirect taxation. The duty on spirits was more than doubled to 30s. a gallon, the duty on a barrel of beer was doubled to 50s. and tobacco tax was raised from 6s. 5d. per pound in 1917, to 8s. 2d. At the same time matches had become a luxury at 2d. a box compared to the pre-war cost of 2d. for a dozen boxes. The dearth of matches effectively limited smokers to six per day but this did mean less mess on the streets and in trains.

The government borrowed money from America and by the start of 1918 was in debt to the sum of $1,860,000,000. By the end of the fourth year of the war, the National Debt was unofficially estimated at £6,629,000,000.

'There were also War Bonds and War Savings Certificates that gave the purchaser a good rate of interest on their capital. As well as individual purchases, it was possible for a town or city to pay the total cost of an aeroplane or tank or any other piece of equipment. To assist in the collection of money from the public there were "Tank Banks" that were sent from town to town and from city to city in competition with each other to see which could raise the most money for the war effort. The sums raised by such methods were large, and when the tanks' appeal started to fade, the government created a ruined French village on Trafalgar Square to raise more money. In total about £600 million was collected by voluntary subscriptions to pay for the war.' Different areas used different names for collecting money but the end result was the same, government War Loans: tank weeks to buy tanks, gun weeks to buy artillery, and cruiser weeks to buy naval vessels. Britain was more successful at raising money than Germany.

Table shows the amount raised using tank banks in early 1918.

City	War loan (£)	City	War loan (£)
Birmingham	6,250,239	Hull	About 2,000,000
Manchester	4,506,000	Leeds	1,521,702
Bradford	4,145,000	Bristol	1,400, 181
London	3,423,264	Sheffield	1,305,761
Newcastle	3,032,324	Cardiff	1,020,800
Liverpool	2,061,012		

In Germany people declared that they were tired of suffering and wanted food and their sons and husbands back. Fear became the predominant emotion and patriotism was dead. So much so that, unlike in Britain and America, there was a reluctance to subscribe to war loans.

Most people had a constant need for extra money to combat rising prices. The London Company of H. Stuart & Co., moleskin specialists, gave advice on how to earn extra income. Simply trap and skin a mole and then dry the fur, for sale at about 10d, three times the pre-war price. They would also buy fox, badger, otter, rabbit and hare skins.

Cities and towns nationally continued to raise smaller sums in the same way as they had done the year before – flag days – but by now they were very well organised and controlled events. In mid-October, the YMCA ran a week-long campaign to raise money for huts.

Probably the most successful organisation at raising funds was the Red Cross. Throughout the war it had relied on voluntary contributions and, by the end of the war, had raised £21,885,035 and spent £20,058,355 'on hospitals, medicine, clothing, grants and care for the sick and wounded'. The money had been raised by donations, collections, a bazaar in Shepherd's Market, two shops in London, church collections, *The Times* Fund, the British Farmers Red Cross Fund, auction sales at Christie's, an auction of wine and spirits, the Gold and Silver Fund, the Dennis-Bayley Fund, the Central PoW Fund, Fresh Air Fund and 'Our Day'.

There was no shortage of coin in Britain, unlike France where the *sou* disappeared and was replaced by local paper money that quickly became unreadable and consequently unusable. In Germany by 1918 most money was paper. Gold had almost vanished and silver had been withdrawn in 1917.

In France, money played a part in the downfall of Paul Marie Bolo, otherwise known as Bolo Pasha. He had cultivated Interior Minister Valpy who was tried for treason and sentenced to five years' imprisonment. Accused of trafficking with the enemy when it was shown that money he used in an attempt to acquire French newspapers came from the Deutsche Bank, he was tried, sentenced to death and shot.

Wars do not stop people committing civilian offences. People continued to get drunk, even though the beer was watered down and in short supply, robberies were committed, even though most able-bodied men were in the army, and far more serious offences were committed. There is no evidence that anywhere in the country was any worse than any other, so the Reading Assizes is probably representative. It opened on 15 October to hear cases of burglary, housebreaking and larceny, bigamy, incest, concealment of birth and wilful murder of a new-born child.

In Berlin the shortages, black-marketing and war-profiteering resulted in a breakdown of order; there was an 'increase in violent crime and thieving, especially of food, which made it hazardous to walk alone in Berlin after dark'.

'There was the usual problem of lost output through industrial unrest, although this had been much reduced during the German offensive in March. By July the workers' patriotic support for the war effort was gone and in that month a strike in an engineering plant in the Midlands was only ended when the government threatened the strikers with conscription.' This was in direct contrast to the words of General Ludendorff, who, on 2 July, said that German workers were 'too reasonable and too patriotic' to ruin the war effort.

In Britain, 'In August, Yorkshire miners, London bus and tram workers, Birmingham and Coventry munitions workers, although they had specifically been asked not to by the government because of the urgent need for ammunition to keep the offensive in France going,' went on strike.

Sir George Ask listed some of the industrial unrest during the year. This included 'trouble on the railways, in pits, gasworks, the cotton industry, flour mills, soap works, the grocery trade, the Post Office, the prisons, the fire brigades, the "co-op" and many other areas. In London bus conductresses claimed the privilege of withdrawing labour. Refuse workers let the rubbish pile up, and when women swept it into heaps they kicked it about the streets again. In Cardiff a soldier who had come home to bury his wife found that he had to dig her grave, since the diggers were on strike; his mates helped him.'

Even the London police joined in (about 14,000 of them, although this was short-lived) demanding higher pay and the recognition of their union (fortunately during their absence from the streets there was no sudden outbreak of crime or unrest). 'The Guards took over in Whitehall and the special police were called out en masse, much to the chagrin of the full-time police. Men in hospital from the front "flung bitter words at the men…and invited them to have a go at the real enemy".' Lloyd George promised them most of what they wanted but not union recognition.

France had similar difficulties. Many workers had grievances and some held revolutionary-pacifist sympathies. To maintain order, four cavalry divisions were held ready to deal with any problems such as the strike at Saint Etienne which was quelled with cavalry and gendarmes. In Britain, strikers were threatened with the army; in France the young strikers were conscripted and older strikers given a pay rise. There were further strikes at the Renault and Citroën plants; both successfully dealt with.

The countryside was a different part of Britain. Food was generally more available in the country than in towns and cities. Across the country, forests were being felled and the landscape transformed. On the coast each new tide washed up wreckage and bodies. The great country houses were experiencing financial problems with many of them having to sell the house contents to meet their tax requirements and death duties. The Reverend Reeve recorded in his journal that 'a large number of estates continue to be put on the market in all parts of the country… Stondon Manor and farms will come under the hammer, I understand, early in July.' The wealthy were also paying for their part in the war.

Both Paris and London suffered badly from air raids during the year but Paris also suffered from very-long-range shelling from large-calibre artillery. The first major raid on the city was on 30 January. On a clear moonlit night 50 Gotha bombers dropped bombs causing 259 casualties. The next day many Parisians left the city for safer areas. More raids followed; the raids in March killed 120.

'Air-raid precautions were intensified, with sandbags protecting important sites and monuments like the Arc de Triomphe,' and communal shelters were set up in every street. As a result, 'cellar life became an institution'. Then on 23 March the Germans started long-range shelling of the city.

As no planes could be seen, everyone was confused. Although the first shell had landed at 7.30 am, the sirens did not sound until 9.15 am. The all-clear was at 2.30 pm. When Parisians left their shelters they found that there had been twenty-five mysterious detonations, a few buildings had been damaged, twenty-five people had been wounded and sixteen killed. The next day they found out that there were no planes involved and that the guns responsible were still a long way away from Paris.

The shelling continued until 9 August. The worst single day was 29 March, Good Friday, when a shell landed on the crowded church of St-Gervais-et-St-Protais, killing eighty-eight of the congregation. Fortunately the overall casualties and damage for the 44 days were comparatively small: 256 killed and 625 wounded. However, this did not stop 500,000 leaving the capital during April; schoolchildren were evacuated and banks sent their records and securities to safer areas. Government departments even began disposing of documents.

In Britain few bombs were dropped in the country; those that did were usually mistakes caused by poor navigation, wishful thinking, mistaken identity or simply a need to jettison weight. While the Zeppelin threat had receded, it did not go away. There were a further four Zeppelin raids before the end of the war: over Norfolk, the Midlands and the north east, resulting in sixteen deaths and seventy-eight people injured. A far greater menace came from the Gothas and Giants that targeted London and the Home Counties. The first raid of the year by these planes was to be the worst.

On 28 January, using a full moon, thirteen Gothas and a Giant flew towards the capital, taking off in thick mist that did not dissipate as they approached England. Six turned back over the North Sea and of the remainder, only three Gothas and the Giant, were able to penetrate the London defences. The other four Gothas bombed Ramsgate, Sheerness and Folkestone where there were no casualties. The aircraft that bombed London caused heavy casualties, 67 killed and 166 injured. Of the fatalities and injuries, the majority were the result of three incidents.

'Londoners were still not accustomed to the sound of warning maroons and when they were fired on the evening of 28 January many people mistook them for bombs. There had already been an air raid alert and crowds were waiting for the Bishopsgate railway goods depot to open; it was an officially designated air-raid shelter. When one of the gates was partly opened there was a frantic rush for the shelter. One person is believed to have tripped and other people fell over the prostrate body. Suddenly there was a heap of struggling, fighting men, women and children. Some were suffocated; others were pushed inescapably against the wall. The entrance was blocked.' And 'by a tragic coincidence there was a similar collective panic at Mile End Underground station in the East End. The casualties were unbelievably small: the total for both places was only fourteen dead and fourteen injured…but the greatest tragedy of the night took place at Long Acre, north of the Strand. The Gothas had gone, but at midnight there was another alarm as the lone Giant flew towards the capital. It was the biggest of them all, R. 39, and it dropped a 660 lb bomb outside Odhams Printing Works. The missile exploded under the pavement and the three-storey building shuddered under the impact. Fire took hold of newsprint reels in the basement. A wall collapsed and overturned printing presses.' There were more than 500 people sheltering in the basement that only had one open exit. 'Amid the flames and smoke of burning newsreels and the danger of being drowned by the water from the fire hoses, people fought and clawed their way towards the one exit. An entrance was made for doctors to give anaesthetics, do some amputations and relieve the worst of the injuries caused by the panic…At the end of it all, thirty-eight people were dead and eighty-five injured.'

Only one other raid came close to causing this much damage during the year. On the penultimate raid of the last year of the war, 23 Gothas and 3 Giants dropped 159 bombs on London, Southend, Ramsgate, Dover and Rochester. Forty-nine people were killed and 177 injured. The damage was estimated at £170,000.

The next night 'three Giant and three or four smaller machines' bombed Kent, Essex and the outskirts of London, killing ten and injuring ten.

Paris was the next target for the bombers. The raid on 30 January, the first aeroplane attack in force on the city, was a reprisal attack, the Germans admitted, for the French bombing of open German towns. The attacks on Britain were intended to keep machines away from the Western Front.

'In February, aeroplane raids were reported on three successive nights – the 16th, 17th and 18th. None were large scale and were mostly frustrated by the London defences.' The raid on the 17th by a single Giant aeroplane was the most deadly. 'It was responsible in all for killing twenty-one persons and injuring thirty-two others.' March brought a further three raids. One came on the 7th in the southern counties and killed twenty-three and injured thirty-nine, and on the 12th, one died from shock. In the second raid of the night eight were killed and thirty-nine injured.

The attack on 19 May, on the evening of Whit-Sunday was the final major effort by the German bombers. In clear still weather 13 aircraft dropped over 10,000Kg of bombs on Essex, Kent and London, killing 49 and injuring 177. Five attackers were brought down by the defences. Paris continued to be bombed after this date and after the last raid on Britain. The final attack on Britain was on 5 August, when all bombs dropped in the sea and one plane was brought down forty miles from land.

'Just to add to the nation's problems there came the great influenza pandemic that killed more people across the world in the space of a year than the war did in its entirety.' It spread quickly and the death toll rose with it, from the 30 people who died from an unidentified illness in Yorkshire and Lancashire in June to over 4,000 a week at the end of October. 'Mostly they died in their beds, suffocating slowly, but some dropped in the street and fields.' Hospitals became so full that they no longer admitted ordinary patients. People wore face masks in the streets and in some towns disinfectant was sprinkled on the roads. Patent medicines had no effect but were widely advertised.

Fortunately, and probably randomly, some areas were worse hit than others. London suffered far more than places like Hull or Reading and not just because of its size. While both suffered, Reading did not lose a whole family and the October outbreak was over in just a week, although it caused schools to close, places of amusement to be placed out of bounds and businesses to double workloads to maintain services. While the epidemic was severe in Hull, the number of deaths was not as high in many towns and cities.

The British population faced 3 waves of the disease and by May 1919 somewhere between 150,000 and 230,000 people were dead, many of them young and previously healthy: most died not from the flu but from the pneumonia that followed. The older population were not as badly affected because they were immune from previous exposure to a similar virus when they were young. Ernest Cooper recorded: 'by the latter part of Oct and early November it [the flu] was raging and several deaths occurred. One woman was quite well at noon and dead next morning, whole families were in bed at once and it spread in the most wholesale manner…my neighbour Docura of the Red Lion kept about with it too long then went to bed and was dead in no time, a fine strong man.'

The virulence of Spanish Flu and the rapidity of death are amply illustrated by a Hull and Reading case. Esther Cooper returned home from work complaining of feeling unwell: 'I think I have got a touch of the influenza, I do feel poorly.' After eating a meal she fell asleep in a chair. Some while later she was found dead. She was 37 years old. Charles Ing, a veteran of 23 with weak lungs caused by gassing at the front, died on Sunday, 27 October, in London. The next day his mother and fiancée Daisy returned to Bracknell. On Tuesday Daisy went into Reading to buy mourning clothes. Returning home she was taken ill and died before 8 o'clock in the morning on Wednesday at her fiancé's house. They were buried in the same grave after a joint funeral.

A similar and equally poignant story concerned a family of three in Hull. The husband contracted influenza, and the wife, who was recovering from her confinement, cared for him, thereby giving the disease to her child. All three died.

The illness seriously affected daily life, with many places being closed, such as schools due to a lack of staff and/or pupils. The entry for one school reads, '21 November – the attendance has become worse owing to influenza, 22 November – School dismissed for indefinite period.' So many people were dying that undertakers were unable to deal with the situation and once again the army had to be called in to help. Taking Sunderland as a typical city the death toll was so great that the Mayor held several conferences a day with funeral directors to hear reports of the situation, and at churches and cemeteries around the city the funeral corteges were kept in queues. In total around three-quarters of the population were affected by this new disease. Milkmen reported the deaths of their customers: in some houses there were many: six dead in a Camberwell house, eight in Stoke Newington. Among the dead were servicemen, at home recovering. One famous death was Captain Leefe Robinson VC, who was famous for shooting down a Zeppelin at Cuffley.

There was no cure as it was a virus but the public were given advice by the government on limiting its spread. It was basically common sense. The public were told to constantly ventilate bedrooms and living rooms; avoid overcrowded rooms and places of amusement; not to sleep in a room with an infected person; not to spit as it spread the disease; not to work too hard and not to be an alcoholic, and finally to regard all catarrhal attacks, and every illness with a rise in temperature, as infectious and adopt appropriate measures at once. Although everyone knew that doctors could do very little, this did not stop people visiting them. During the October outbreak, one surgery in West Reading reported that when the waiting room was full, a queue formed in the street that must have been at least 70 yards long.

In South Africa, the dead littered the streets, boxed in orange crates and packing cases, with great stacks on railway platforms. Visiting ships stayed at a safe distance and anchored in Table Bay, and soldiers could be seen digging graves and knocking coffins together. This also happened in Woolwich where undertakers had to call in troops to help make coffins.

As the German offensive to end the war faltered, civilian morale rose and fell according to distance and nationality. With the Allied success in August, Allied confidence and expectation rose and German Home Front morale fell: 'the public sank into yet deeper depression, filled with one wish: to end the war.' The collapse of Home Front morale was hastened by the Allied use of propaganda which Hindenburg believed was poisoning the home. With ever worsening news from the various fronts it was no longer possible to 'hide the truth of Germany's predicament' and on 2 October a representative of the High Command told a meeting of Reichstag members that Hindenburg and Ludendorff had decided to tell the Kaiser that the war must be ended. Coupled with the Kaiser's decision to allow greater power-sharing and the appointment of a liberal-minded Chancellor, change was on the way, even democracy. The next day the new Chancellor sent an armistice proposal to President Wilson. It was rejected because as the German Army withdrew it was 'carrying out systematic deportation and destruction'. On 10 October U-boats sank 2 passenger ships with the loss of over 800 lives. The newly upbeat population who had felt peace arriving, sank back into gloom.

On 23 October the socialist Karl Leibknecht was released after two years in prison and immediately went to the Russian Embassy in a flower-bedecked carriage. There were growing threats of disorder and a populist view that the Kaiser must go. This could be traced back to January's distribution of illegal leaflets in the back streets of Berlin proclaiming 'Down with the Kaiser: Down with the Government'. Now even children were saying the Kaiser must go, as Princess Blücher noted. But before the Kaiser went, Ludendorff resigned and Austria sued for peace. The German government sent, on 27 October, a fourth Note asking for armistice proposals.

In early November the Kiel mutiny precipitated further troubles; the 'revolt spread swiftly to Lübeck, Hamburg, Cuxhaven, and Bremen. By the 8th there was rioting at Cologne, Düsseldorf, Coblenz and Mainz.' In an attempt to halt Germany sliding into chaos and civil war, the Chancellor took it upon himself to announce the Emperor's abdication, proposing a regency, the Socialist Friedrich Ebert as Chancellor and a bill for a general election. The abdication was met with wild rejoicing and in many cities and towns the national flag was replaced by the Red Flag. 'Crowds of soldiers, sailors, men, women and children packed the streets [of Berlin], interspersed with lorry-loads of cheering, flag-waving servicemen.' Although there was sporadic shooting and violence when officers were attacked, generally it suggested a 'victory rather than the culmination of Germany's defeat'. Perhaps for many it was a victory?

The Allies had already made war preparations for 1919 and even though the public had been following the slow and steady collapse of the Central Powers, the end of the war came as a surprise. One wonders why, when, the day before, the *News of the World* published headlines like 'The war is won – Victory is ours; German Army crashes into ruins; Fires of revolution sweep the land; Retreat becoming a rout'. True to form, *The Times* announced the end of the war as it had the beginning, in single-column headlines.

At 11 am, the maroons were fired in London (the air raid signal) and Big Ben and local church bells sounded out spontaneously after their enforced silence. Ignoring the restrictions, newspaper bills reappeared to announce that fighting had ceased on all fronts. Crowds streamed out into the streets, screaming and shouting with joy. A ticker-tape style welcome to the peace was provided by thousands of official forms being thrown into the streets. Everybody gave up work for the day to celebrate. Boy Scouts ran through the streets sounding the 'All Clear' on their bugles as they had done throughout the war. The sound of cheering, hand bells ringing, and police whistles blowing was cacophonous. People danced in Trafalgar Square and a bonfire, playfully lit by Dominion troops, permanently scarred the plinth of Nelson's column.

Shortly after the news of the armistice became known, thousands gathered in front of Buckingham Palace to cheer and see the King and Queen as they had done on 4 August 1914, but this time not to cheer for the war. Several times during the day the King and Queen appeared on the palace balcony to acknowledge the enthusiastic greeting of the assembled throng. *The Times* reported that after the King's first appearance on the balcony, people turned to go, but were met by fresh throngs, flushed with enthusiasm. Through Green Park came a procession of munitions girls in their overalls, carrying a very large Union Jack. 'Men with flags tied to sticks and umbrellas, women who had wreathed their hats with the national colours, Dominion soldiers, officers, and men of British regiments, troops from the United States, men of the Royal Air Force, Wrens, W.A.A.C.s, girls from Government offices, and children, poured into the wide open space before the palace railings. Motor-lorries brought along cheering loads of passengers, some in uniform and some civilians. Motor-cars carried three and four times their normal number of people. Every taxi-cab had half-a-dozen men and girls on the roof, and soldiers tried to keep precarious places on the steps. Everybody seemed to have a flag, and some of these bore the words "Welcome Home". Australian soldiers climbed up the marble carving of the Victoria memorial, and secured observation posts in this way high above the heads of the crowd. Admirals and generals joined the throng, which by noon had become a wonderful surging multitude, stretching far up the Mall.'

Patriotic songs were sung, and at short intervals soldiers led the calls of 'We want King George'. When palace servants hung festoons of crimson velvet over the balcony it was obvious that the

King was going to appear. During the long wait, a band of junior army officers, carrying flags and blowing police whistles, pushed into the massed people, cleared a circle, and romped hand-in-hand around a teddy bear on wheels decorated with a flag, while an American officer, from the top of a taxi, entertained the crowd with a demonstration of college yells.

The crowd had gathered to see the King, and became more insistent and louder. Just before 1pm the band of the Brigade of Guards came in sight playing a triumphal march. As they wheeled into position in the forecourt, the King stepped out onto the balcony. Also present were the Queen, Princess Mary, Princess Patricia and the Duke of Connaught. According to *The Times History of the War*, 'a roar of cheering went up such as London had not heard during the period of the war, and above the upturned faces handkerchiefs fluttered, hats waved, and thousands of flags, the flags of all the allies, flapped and shook. The strains of the National Anthem, played by the Guards, at first were scarcely heard against the cheering, but gradually the people caught the music and with the third line of the hymn voices took up the words. Came once more "Rule Britannia," and then another tremendous note of cheering, led by the King, while the Queen waved a flag above her head. Next the band led the crowd in singing "Auld Lang Syne," and after this "Tipperary," "Keep the home fires burning," and the more stately, but beautiful, "Land of Hope and Glory." "Tipperary" was accompanied with nervous laughter and tears. People remembered the early days of the war, and emotion gripped and almost overwhelmed many of them. The crowd showed no wish to dissolve, and men began to call for a speech. The band quietened them with "The Old Hundredth," and the crowd reverently took up the hymn. Enthusiasm quickly had its fling again. American and Belgian national airs provoked great cheers, and everybody sang the "Marseillaise." Then the King spoke. Few could hear him, but his message was well chosen. "With you I rejoice, and thank God for the victories which the Allied Armies have won, bringing hostilities to an end and peace within sight." "Now thank we all our God" was played by the band after the King's words, and a historic scene ended with a final round of cheering, in which the musicians of the band and the King joined.'

Quite how many telegrams the King and Queen received offering them congratulations on the victory is unknown, but the one from the people of Sonning, a small village a few miles outside Reading, is probably similar to many. During the evening service held to celebrate the victory, after an emotional speech, the Reverend Gibbs Payne Crawfurd proposed sending a telegram to the King and Queen: 'The people of Sonning, assembled in their Parish church beg in humble and loving loyalty to offer congratulations to the King and Queen on the glorious victory and to thank them for their share in it.' It was duly sent that day. Judging by the speed of reply, sent the next day, the King received few such telegrams or someone else was reading and replying: 'The King and Queen thank you and your parishioners for your message of loyal congratulations upon the victory of the Allies.'

When the crowd eventually dispersed it was to continue the celebrations elsewhere. It was drizzling as dusk fell, but this did not stop the bonfires and torch-lit processions. Searchlights swept the sky giving the city the first night light for a long time. As one man remembered, 'there was a hell of a show all over country. People went mad. All night street parties, with beer and drinks and singing.' The King also celebrated. The Royal cellars were unlocked and a bottle of brandy was opened that had been laid down by George IV to celebrate the Battle of Waterloo; unfortunately it tasted 'very musty'. But while the celebrations went on, for many there was only sorrow; throughout the country thousands queued outside churches to attend thanksgiving services and to pray for the Unreturning Army.

The same sentiments and reactions occurred all over Britain to a greater or lesser extent. In Southwold, Ernest Cooper received a phone call from the County Adjutant to say that the armistice had been signed and that guns were firing and bells ringing in Ipswich. At first he could not take it in, even though the papers had intimated for a couple of days that it could happen very soon. When he arrived at the Mayor's he found that he already knew. A few minutes later a car came in from the local air station full of 'mad officers, cheering, waving flags and blowing trumpets. Flags soon came out, and bells began to ring and a few of us adjourned to the Mayor's house and cracked some bottles of Fizz. An impromptu meeting was called and the Mayor read the official Telegram from the Swan balcony, some soldiers came up on a wagon with the Kaiser in effigy, which they tied to the Town Pump and burnt amidst cheers.'

Not every village knew of the armistice by 11 am; some did not find out until much later in the day. To make sure the outlying villages knew of the armistice, one Reading department store sent a motor delivery van, bedecked with Union Jacks and bunting, to spread the news. Not everywhere was so lucky. The vicar of Stondon Massey in Essex recorded that, while some heard the distant bells at Brentwood, it was not until the afternoon that definite tidings reached the villagers and then it filtered through chiefly in the form of private messages. As soon as he had official confirmation, he allowed the bells to be chimed. He was lucky. In Altrincham, the Rev. Hewlett Johnson had to round 'up five 11-year-old girls from the playing fields'. Leading them to the belfry, he instructed them with hand signals and managed 'an attenuated peal' of sorts. In St. Austell, 'an attempt was made to dance the traditional Floral Dance', which resident A.L. Rowse described as rather pathetic, 'like a gesture remembered from some other existence'.

While 'some towns and villages were simply too tired, or disillusioned, to celebrate', others were not. In the village of Cottingham, the main street, Hallgate, was decorated for a week and on Armistice Day, youths burned an effigy of the Kaiser on the Market Green and set off fireworks.

Reading, in common with a number of other towns, spent a week of rejoicing. When the GWR hooter sounded at 11 am, followed by other hooters, people poured out of offices and shops on the way to Market Place for the official announcement. The hoisting of Sutton's Seeds' flag was the certain sign the war was over. Across the town tools were downed and many were given a half-day paid holiday. One large department store beat the generosity of the other employers and gave all its employees an extra week's salary. The euphoria was such that even German PoWs working in Reading cheered.

In Reading impromptu processions were speedily organised which marched around the town headed by the band of the Royal Berks Depot. The trams stopped at 4 pm giving the whole town to the public to continue celebrating. Street lamps were quickly cleaned and shops and houses removed their shading to increase the light. Bells were rung and fireworks lit. Even the rain did not spoil the moment.

The mass desertion of many from their workplace in Hull was simply described as they 'took holiday' and although there were no arrangements to close schools, many children imitated their parents and also 'took holiday.' As in London and Reading, crowds gathered spontaneously and flags appeared everywhere. The church bells rang and the task of clearing blackout paint from street lights began.

In France, 'on armistice morning the bells and cheers rang out all over' the country, 'in a celebration as wild and jubilant as that of Britain.' That night, 'delirious crowds hauled the German guns from the Place de la Concorde and at the War Ministry the Prime Minister was hailed by a huge concourse roaring "Clemenceau!".'

What struck most were the lights after tea. The world was no longer dim. Shops had been permitted to display lights, some of the street lighting had been scraped clean and public buildings were lit-up. And then there were the fireworks.

Writing for the December edition of the parish magazine, the vicar of Sonning recorded the experience of the end of the war in his village: 'Who of us can ever forget Monday, November 11th, 1918, and the glorious news it has brought us all,' he wrote. 'It had been arranged by notice given from the pulpit on Sunday that when the news reached the village there should be, after the ringing of the bells, an impromptu service of prayer and thanksgiving in the church. The news reached the village chiefly through the hooters in Reading, about 11 a.m. At once some of the ringers rushed to the belfry and set a joyous peal going. Flags were got out everywhere; on the church tower the St. George's flag and the American Stars and Stripes were soon flying; and almost every house in the village had some flag or other flying from it; people were all out in the streets and work went lightly for the time. Notice was sent that the bells would ring again at 6.30 p.m. and that the service in the church would then follow at 7 pm. There were eight men ringing the full peal this time.'

In Woodley the armistice was announced to residents by the hooters of Reading and Wokingham and like its Sonning neighbour the church bells replied and flags soon flew. As in so many churches across the country, an evening service was held. Neither the rain nor the influenza epidemic stopped the parishioners of Woodley from going to the service: the church was nearly filled.

While it was a release for many, the end of the war would for some be anti-climactic: a return to the problems and monotony of before the war or a simply a time of great sadness because of their loss. This was reflected by Huntley and Palmer's in Reading who impressed upon their employees the sorrow as well as the gladness which this occasion brought to the bereaved. Most of their employees stayed at work when the siren blew but, interestingly, many of the female workers stopped at 1 o'clock in the afternoon.

A young girl, Gladys Johnson, recalled her memories of the end of the war. Her father had been sent home after being gassed and wounded in the hand. His experiences gave him terrible nightmares and made him violent. 'He would wake up screaming even before he was taken ill. He was always fighting. Anything that moved, curtains, anything, he'd be getting up to fight. Yet when he wasn't having nightmares, there couldn't be a nicer man...He would go absolutely mad. I can remember it so well towards the end. He was laid in bed for a fortnight and he went raving mad. It was in my mother's bedroom...All she had in there was a full size bed and a gramophone with a big green horn at the window. We never knew why we took it upstairs. But if we had not, my father would have jumped through the window that night. He got out of bed and tried to strangle my mother and me. It ended with the horn going through the window. My neck went black with the marks where he tried to choke me. He died the next day, the day after Armistice Day. We had no Armistice celebrations inside or outside the house.' And to add insult to injury, while his own doctor had been treating him for the effects of poison gas, the 'locum' doctor added to his death certificate a sentence that would lose the widow's pension – 'Not aggravated by war service.'

Although it was Armistice Day, the dead still had to be buried. As the bells rang, Mrs E.L. Davis was burying her husband. After spending two years convalescing, an operation on his head wound killed him.

At this time in London, 1,000 died of influenza, and across the country thousands more lay ill or were dying. Francis Chichester, lying on the sanatorium floor at Marlborough College, noted that there was cheering outside and only a few died that day.

For Ernest Read the last day of the war was dampened by sadness: 'The only sad event was poor Docura's funeral which took place with Military Honours in the afternoon...doubly sad that a man of 37 and a keen volunteer from the start should be buried amidst the Armistice rejoicings.'

The financial cost of the influenza pandemic is clearly demonstrated by the returns of the Prudential Assurance Company. It paid more than twice as much during the eight-week epidemic, on account of deaths from influenza, than it paid out in war claims:

Type of claim	Cost in Pounds
Influenza	620,000
War	279,000

In France, until Clemenceau's son-in-law died of the disease in mid-October, all mention of the infection had been rigorously controlled. At that time it was killing around 1,200 people a week in Paris. To keep up with the deaths, funerals were being conducted as late as midnight.

Small villages, though relatively isolated, were not immune. Woodley, a small Berkshire village, while celebrating the armistice also noted the death of one of its sons in action on 1 November and three deaths caused by flu. The village school was closed for three weeks to contain the infection.

Death was omnipresent for a host of reasons. Across Britain, parents and wives received the dreaded yellow envelope with the Army Council's regrets on the loss of their loved one. Unfortunately, 'there were great wads of telegrams still to be dispatched.'

Echoing the thoughts of Huntley and Palmer's, the writer QT cautioned people not to forget those who were grieving: 'In the hour of our triumph let us not for one moment forget the heroic dead, the gallant men to whose imperishable renown we owe the defeat of our deadly foes and the safety of civilisation…the dead and the thousands of maimed who saved England and civilisation.'

During the war many had turned to *The Bible* for comfort and solace. People had gone to church but services at the end and shortly after the war were generally better attended. On the Sunday following the armistice the vicar of Woodley church noted that services were very well attended and it was obvious among the congregation that the clouds of war had broken and that it was 'the dawning of a just and righteous peace'. The sermon that evening was based Psalm cxxiv. 7: 'We have escaped like a bird from the fowler's snare; the snare has been broken, and we have escaped.'

Throughout this series of books, mention has been made of some of the families who had many members fighting. QT asked the reader to have sympathy for all those who suffered a loss, and to have a greater regard for those who had suffered multiple losses. He was referring to the losses felt in the Reading area: the ex-Mayor of the town had lost four of his five sons, and the Loder-Symonds family had lost four sons and a daughter who was drowned when the *Galway Castle* sank in September 1918; his wife and another daughter also died. Across the country, many families had suffered multiple losses. In Barnard Castle, the Smiths mourned for five sons and, prefiguring *Saving Private Ryan*, Mrs Smith had written to the Queen appealing for her sixth son to be taken out of harm's way. Weeks later she received the reply she had wanted: he would be posted from the front and stationed as near to Barnard Castle as possible on compassionate grounds. The Beechey family lost five of their eight sons; the Soul family lost five to the fighting, and, in a cruel twist of fate their only surviving son died of meningitis soon after the war. In Canada, Charlotte Wood had five sons killed and two seriously injured.

But for the majority, it was the war to end all wars and a return to the peace that they had bought at any price, quietly forgetting that Britain was still fighting against the Bolsheviks and there were troubles in the Middle East and on the north-west frontier of India. It was only an armistice; genuine peace would come later, but even so, most thought of demobilisation and repatriation. The latter group were to be the first home. And in just a few weeks it would be Christmas.

Although there was no fighting, only a small number of men would initially be released in case the Germans reneged on the arrangements for their withdrawal. As with previous war-Christmases, this meant money was needed to supply the troops with a memorable time and the hope that it would be the last of the war. While organisations started to wind down their activities, regimental charities could not. Once again the need was for money.

'Now the war was over, the next general election could take place. Changes in voting rights and boundary re-organisation made it more unpredictable than previous elections.' Vote counting would be delayed because of the many new voters serving with the armed forces. How many more people were entitled to vote is clearly shown by the numbers of voters in the Reading area and can be taken as representative: 45,379 compared to 11,200 pre-war.

The first returning PoWs arrived at Hull to a hearty welcome on the SS *Archangel,* on 17 November. By Christmas nearly 39,000 men had landed at Hull. The arrival of the PoWs was good news for most families but sad for others. Many now faced the realisation that a loved one reported missing would not be returning. This was shown by the births and deaths columns in the papers: 'previously reported missing, now known to have been killed on or about…' – the dates differed but the feelings were the same; a final realisation.

Probably not unique but certainly uncommon was the fate of Walter George. He had been confirmed killed in October by a death telegram and a letter from both the Paymaster and the Graves Director. On the same day they received his grave number in France, his family received a letter from him. It was not a delayed letter written before his death, but one telling them he was wounded and in a PoW camp. A few days later he was home.

Not everyone received such positive news before Christmas. Illustrating the fact that the pandemic was worldwide, George Smart received the sad news his daughter in Canada had just died of pneumonia following flu, leaving a week-old baby and two other small children. Influenza deaths continued to be registered as did the deaths of soldiers. For many weeks after the armistice the casualty lists continued to appear, listing those who died through disease, accidents and from wounds received weeks or months before.

Although the war had finished, goods did not suddenly become available again. Householders were urged to exercise 'the utmost economy in the burning of fuel and light' as they did during the war because there would be a continued insufficiency of coal. However, as all ships now arrived, there was more certainty about food, in particular meat. The purchase value of a meat coupon rose 25 per cent and there was still a shortage of British beef but fortunately other meats came off ration, so customers could buy as much as they wished. Foods like suet, fat, edible offal, imported tender loins and stripped bones were freely available.

As the armistice looked certain to become a peace, companies and organisations began to report on their war: what they had done, how much they had produced and, of course, and most important, their roll of honour detailing casualties, numbers served and honours received – not always correctly. Reading School listed 74 deaths among the 425 who served, but a month later gave the total as 77 out of 418. When the school memorial was unveiled it listed 82 deaths, omitting 2 for some unknown reason. This was to be the case across the country when names for memorials were listed.

In Britain and the Allied countries, the returning men were given a great welcome. As a defeated nation how did things differ in Germany? Captain Sulzbach, returning with his men to Bonn, was pleased with the reception he met. They were greeted by crowds that 'cheered like anything' when they marched past their commanding general at the bridge over the Rhine. They were returning to a Germany riven with political discontent and violence. Not long after their arrival in the homeland, they would be followed by the Allies who were moving to take up their specified bridgeheads and occupy Germany up to the Rhine. The first troops arrived at Aachen on 24 November; it was the beginning of the occupation of Germany. In the occupied areas, civil life would be controlled by the military, in much the same way as the Germans had done for the last four years across much of Europe. It would however be much more benevolent.

While the German Army was retiring, the German High Seas Fleet was leaving dock for the last time. At Harwich on 20 November people watched the arrival of U-boats and a week later the larger vessels could be seen heading into Scapa Flow.

Suddenly it was Christmas: a special one, it was extended to three days. Necessarily touched with pathos it was one most people wanted to remember. The Post Office was phenomenally busy as were the shops who reported an exceptionally busy time. Money was plentiful but, where the goods suddenly came from, after wartime shortages, is unclear. Certainly toy sales outstripped supply. Big department stores broke all previous records. The labour shortage still had an effect: a lack of bottling staff meant a shortage of wine; a shortage of trawler men meant less fish, and the lack of labour in the fishing ports meant there was insufficient smoked fish. However, most ate well, especially in the work houses and military hospitals, and tried to make the most of it. The wounded soldiers were treated not just to a good meal but, as in previous years, to a range of entertainments.

The King sent a message to all the wounded still in hospital waiting to go home: 'Another Christmas has come round, and we are no longer fighting. God has blessed our efforts, and the Queen and I offer you our hearty good wishes for a happy Christmas, and many bright years to come…'

On Christmas Eve, the *Hull Daily Mail* wrote that the rosy sunshine gave it the potential to be 'the Greatest Christmas since the first'. Afterwards the *Hull Times* wrote that it was the happiest since the war broke out. Certainly shopkeepers and traders were happy.

'There was much to look forward to in the New Year, the return of loved ones being foremost for most families. Rationing would end and sporting fixtures would restart.' The number of horse racing fixtures would be the same as 1914.

'With no war, restrictions on celebrations were fewer, allowing New Year festivities.' Across the country there were 'noisy manifestations of rejoicing…at midnight'. In most places there was an attempt to return to pre-war times, although most knew this could not happen. Bells rang out, buzzers rang out the all-clear, and churches and chapels were filled with larger congregations than usual. Few, if any, would have disagreed with the vicar of Woodley's comment during the 17 November evening service: 'God grant that the tyranny of war may be past for all time.'

Within hours of the New Year, the first disaster struck. HMS *Iolaire* hit the infamous rocks, The Beasts of Holm, and eventually sank: officially 205 men perished but as there was no list of passengers, it could have been higher. The continuing casualty lists would for many make the newly-won peace hollow.

Section 1

Recruitment and departure

GWI-HF_6 Newly drafted men at Camp Deven, Massachusetts, undergoing their first examination.

GWI-HF_7 New recruits undergoing basic training somewhere in one of the new army camps in America.

GWI-HF_8 At the foot of the statue of Liberty, Captain Bealey of the RAF is addressing American officers and men about to start for Europe.

GWI-HF_10 Just turned 18 and in uniform. The writer's maternal grandfather was conscripted in August 1918 and about to go to France when the war ended. He was demobilised on 11 November as surplus to requirements but volunteered as a regular the same day and quickly found himself in India.

GWI-HF_9 The King is saluting and being saluted by American troops as they march past the Royal party in front of Buckingham Palace.

GWI-HF_11 Heavy officer casualties meant that many men from the ranks were promoted. These are four hopefuls training at 2 OCB (Pembroke College, Cambridge) to be infantry officers.

GWI-HF_13 Two new recruits for the WRENs (Women's Royal Naval Service) completing the compulsory paperwork.

Officers' Kit

FOR FRANCE

OFFICERS just taking up their Commissions from Cadet Battalions will find the following list of great service. The articles included are those recommended by the Army Council as being absolutely necessary. They are additional to the kit already issued to the Officer Cadets, and to articles such as Revolvers, etc., which are obtainable from Ordnance.

		£	s.	d.
1	Service Cap	0	14	6
1	Whipcord Service Jacket ..	4	10	0
1	pair ,, ,, Slacks ..	1	18	6
1	pair Bedford Cord Breeches	2	10	0
1	British Warm	4	4	0
1	Trench Coat	3	10	0
1	pair Marching Boots ..	2	5	0
1	Wolseley Valise with Name and Regiment painted on	3	11	9
1	Sleeping Bag (Kapok) ..	1	15	0
1	Haversack with Sling and Swivels	0	16	6
1	Aluminium Water Bottle ..	0	15	6
1	Lanyard and Whistle ..	0	2	6
1	Service Hussif	0	2	11
1	Hold-all	0	6	6
1	(Combination) Knife, Fork and Spoon	0	6	6
1	Enamel Cup	0	1	0
1	Field Service Pocket Book..	0	1	0
1	Map Case	0	16	6
1	Bucket	0	4	6
		£28	**12**	**2**

TERMS—NET CASH.

Kits completed and Uniforms made to measure in 24 hours.

Military Catalogue post free on request.

GAMAGES

The Headquarters of Military Outfitting.

HOLBORN LONDON
—— E.C. 1 ——

WOUNDED OFFICERS

We are always pleased to send a representative to any London Hospital to take instructions for New Kit.

GWI-HF_12 Officers had to buy their own uniforms and equipment from a government grant which covered the basics at a low level. Quality uniform and kit cost considerably more. Gamages was one of the larger suppliers.

GWI-HF_14 WRENs in training: a squad at physical drill.

GWI-HF_16 RAF aircrew officers undergoing training in the Great Hall at University College, Reading.

GWI-HF_15 A female member of the newly-formed RAF. This enlisted woman has volunteered for service only as an immobile, that is, she would only serve in her home area, so if she lived in Cardiff she would only work on airfields around the city.

GWI-HF_17 Admiral Sir Rosslyn Wemyss KCB, First Sea Lord, inspecting units of the Boys' Naval Brigade on the Horse Guards in May 1918.

GWI-HF_18 Admiral Wemyss is speaking to one of the youngest of the boys of the brigade, which in the first three years of the war had sent over a thousand boys both to the navy and army, and five hundred into the Mercantile Marine.

GWI-HF_19 A number of conscripts, although perfectly healthy and fit to fight were assigned to service in the United Kingdom because they were of German descent. The men here are the 30th Middlesex Regiment who were stationed in Reading. They were known as the Kaiser's Own because of their German origins.

Section 2

Home Defence, Raids & U-boats

GWI-HF_20 The public reception at Southampton of a thousand American soldiers, some of the survivors from the transport *Tuscania* which was torpedoed off the Irish coast on 5 February 1918. Of the 2,397 people aboard, 210 lost their lives.

GWI-HF_21 Friends of those on board the *Tuscania* are seen arriving at the Anchor Company's offices in Glasgow for news.

GWI-HF_22 Survivors of the torpedoed hospital ship *Rewa* that was sunk in the Bristol Channel on 4 January.

GWI-HF_23 By 1918 London was ringed with defences. The picture shows men of the RNAS AAC practising bringing their gun into action.

GWI-HF_24 Mobile guns were used to provide anti-aircraft defence.

GWI-HF_22A As HMHS *Rewa* took approximately two hours to sink, there was sufficient time to get all the wounded and ship's crew onto the lifeboats. Casualties were light: four engine men died in the initial explosion.

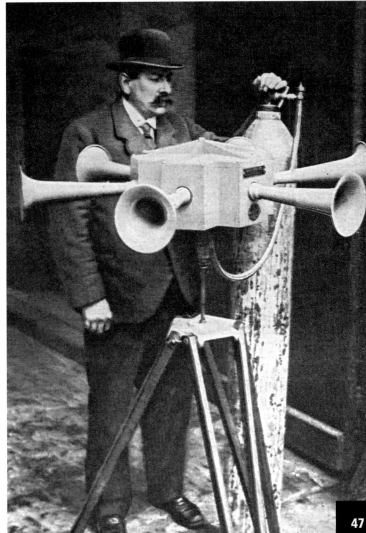

GWI-HF_25 This French six-horn air-raid siren worked on compressed air.

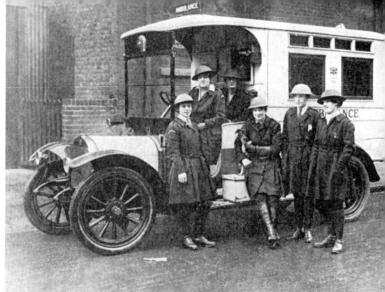

GWI-HF_28 Air raid casualties in London were rapidly transported to hospital by London County Council ambulances. The crews were usually women.

GWI-HF_26 A hand-cranked siren commonly used in French munition-works, magazines and aviation camps.

GWI-HF_27 As the threat of air-raids increased, Parisian monuments were protected to prevent damage from blast and shrapnel. These are the *Chevaux de Marly* on the Place de la Concorde in specially constructed wooden shelters.

GWI-HF_29 The largest sirens were placed on rooftops in Paris.

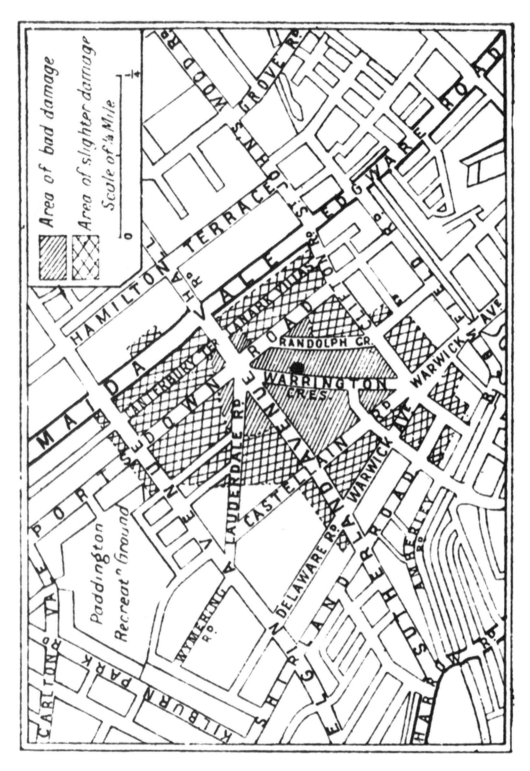

GWI-HF_30 On 7 March, a single 1,000kg bomb dropped on Warrington Crescent by an aircraft 'pulverised four houses and broke the glass of almost a thousand others.' Twelve people died and over twenty were injured. Map shows the area damaged by just one bomb.

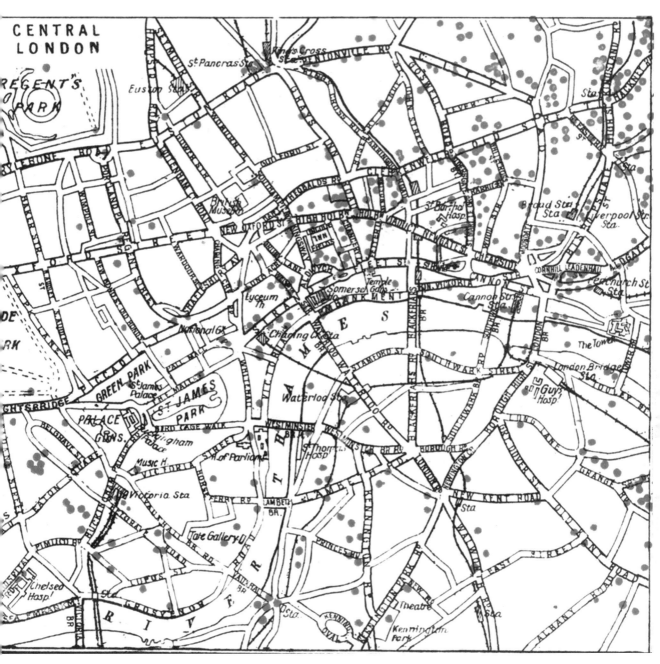

GWI-HF_31 A map based on the fire brigades of the London area showing where bombs fell on Central London.

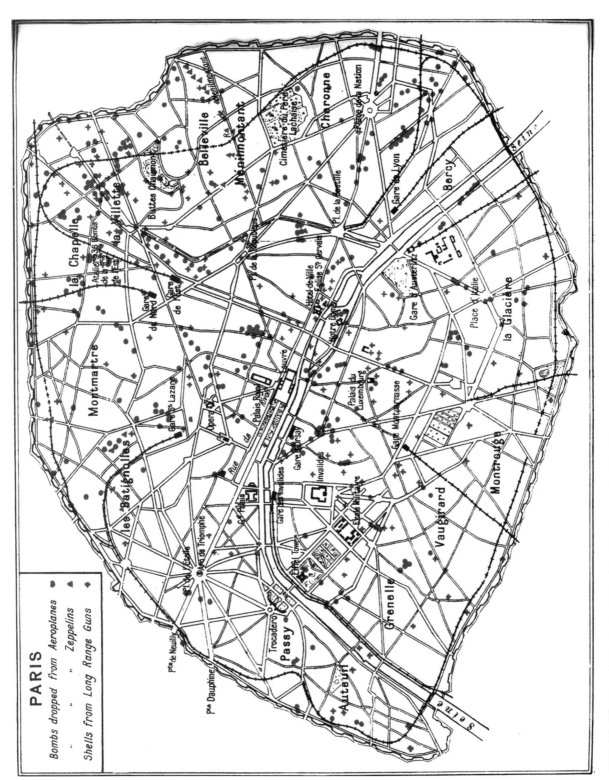

GWI-HF_32 A plan of Paris showing the localities hit by German aircraft and long-range guns.

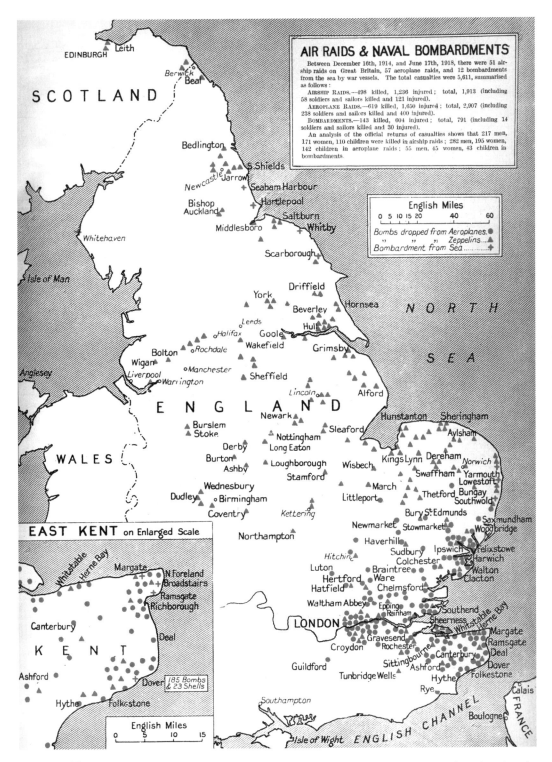

AIR RAIDS & NAVAL BOMBARDMENTS

Between December 16th, 1914, and June 17th, 1918, there were 51 airship raids on Great Britain, 57 aeroplane raids, and 12 bombardments from the sea by war vessels. The total casualties were 5,611, summarised as follows :

AIRSHIP RAIDS.—498 killed, 1,236 injured ; total, 1,913 (including 58 soldiers and sailors killed and 121 injured).

AEROPLANE RAIDS.—619 killed, 1,650 injured ; total, 2,907 (including 238 soldiers and sailors killed and 400 injured).

BOMBARDMENTS.—143 killed, 604 injured ; total, 791 (including 14 soldiers and sailors killed and 30 injured).

An analysis of the official returns of casualties shows that 217 men, 171 women, 110 children were killed in airship raids ; 282 men, 195 women, 142 children in aeroplane raids ; 55 men, 45 women, 43 children in bombardments.

English Miles

0 5 10 15 20   40   60

Bombs dropped from Aeroplanes.......●
  "   "   "   Zeppelins.......▲
Bombardment from Sea...........✠

EAST KENT on Enlarged Scale

185 Bombs & 23 Shells

English Miles

0   5   10   15

GWI-HF_33 A chart showing the exact localities in England and Scotland that suffered from hostile aircraft attacks and naval bombardment between 16 December 1914 to 17 June 1918.

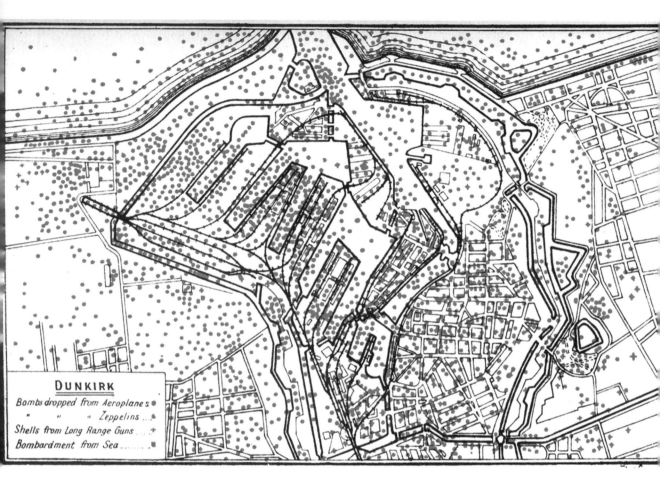

DUNKIRK

Bombs dropped from Aeroplanes .....●

" " " Zeppelins .....●

Shells from Long Range Guns .....+

Bombardment from Sea .....■

GWI-HF_34 A map of Dunkirk showing where bombs were dropped by planes and Zeppelins and where shells from long-range guns and German naval ships fell. Compare the density with London and Paris.

NATIONAL
AIR RAID
DISTRESS
FUND

GWI-HF_35 In Britain the answer to every problem seemed to be a Flag Day. This was sold to raise funds for the National Air Raid Distress Fund.

GWI-HF_36 As Britain's air defences improved, the number of planes shot down increased. This is the wreckage of a Gotha G V bomber brought down by Captain George Henry Hackwill MC. This was the first victory ever achieved in combat between aircraft at night.

GWI-HF_37 During 1918, the British bombing offensive against Germany increased and British planes suffered more casualties. This is a Handley Page O/400 that crashed near Metz.

GWI-HF_38 This Gotha bomber was shot down near Zuydcoote on the coast during a raid on Dunkirk. The crew were captured before they could destroy the craft and it was placed on display in front of Jean Bart's statue in Jean Bart Place.

GWI-HF_39 A Gotha aircraft brought down in Belgium by Belgian anti-aircraft gunners.

GWI-HF_40 Crowds of sightseers at the crash site of a Gotha bomber on 19 May 1918.

GWI-HF_41 On 11 April 1918 the Germans shelled Paris. One shell landed in a ward in a maternity hospital.

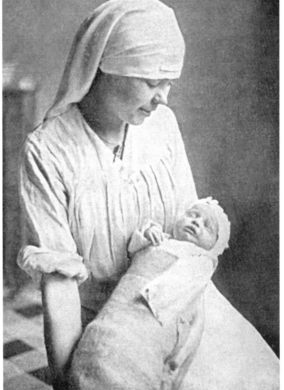

GWI-HF_42 Pictured is a casualty from the shelling of the maternity hospital. The baby lost an arm.

GWI-HF_43 The Royal Hospital in Chelsea suffered damage during a raid on the night of 16/17 February.

GWI-HF_44 A bomb crater in the middle of Rue Drouot after the raid on Paris on the night of 8 March.

GWI-HF_45 The result of a 300kg bomb dropped on the Rue de Rivoli on the night of 12 April.

GWI-HF_46 On the night of 30 January, Broca Hospital, on Rue Broca, was hit by a 50kg bomb.

GWI-HF_47 A 50kg bomb hit No. 119 Rue Saint-Antoine on the night of 12 April.

GWI-HF_51 Paris was shelled on 13 April. Two shells fell on number 4 Rue Saint-Georges and 43 and 45 Rue de la Victoire. The third shell fell on number 35 Rue Saint-Georges which is pictured here.

GWI-HF_48 German soldiers and civilians investigating the results of a British bomber attack.

GWI-HF_49 The Père Lachaise cemetery was hit by a long-range shell on 25 March 1918.

GWI-HF_53 On 28 January the printing works of Odhams in Long Acre, London, was bombed by two Gotha bombers. The building was used as an air-raid shelter and 38 people were killed and 85 injured.

GWI-HF_54 A shell from the 'Paris Gun' hit the church of St. Gervais on 29 March during the Good Friday morning service. The roof collapsed killing 88 people and injuring 68. This was the worst single incident of civilian loss during the bombardment.

Amiens bombardé en 1918
Intérieur de la Maison du Docteur D...,
Boulevard du Mail

GWI-HF_55 Amiens was also subject to long distance shelling. This shows a house in the Boulevard du Mail.

GWI-HF_58 Three victims of the air raid during the night of 30/31 January. The two children, Lucien and Marcelle, were killed and their mother severely wounded. The day after the raid, their father came home for ten days' leave.

GWI-HF_57 This photo shows the effect of a British bomb on the museum in Trier.

GWI-HF_59 The funeral of Lucien and Marcelle was of national interest.

GWI-HF_60 Along the route to the cemetery the roads were lined with thousands of onlookers.

Section 3

Casualty and Captivity

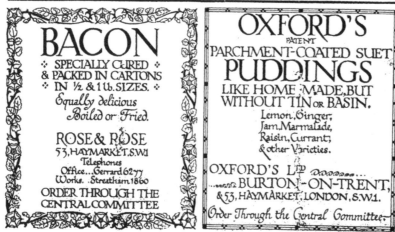

THE BRITISH PRISONER OF WAR

The Monthly Journal of the Central Prisoners of War Committee of the British Red Cross and Order of St. John.

Vol. I.—No. 8   AUGUST, 1918   [Per annum, direct. 4/-, including postage.]   Price Fourpence

SMOKES FOR PRISONERS OF WAR

300 Wills' "Woodbines" Cigarettes, in packets of 5	3/11	
300 Wills' "Gold Flakes" ,, in packets of 10 ...	6/3	
300 Player's Navy Cut ,, in packets of 10 ...	6/3	
300 Wills' "Three Castles" ,, in packets of 10 ...	7/5	
½ lb. Wills' "Capstan" Navy Cut Tobacco, in ¼ lb. tins ...	2/6	
½ lb. Player's Navy Cut Tobacco, in ¼ lb. tins	2/6	

Can only forward 300 cigarettes, or ½ lb. of tobacco each two weeks, to one man.

Wills' "Woodbine" Cigarettes, in packets of 10	12/0 per 1,000
Wills' "Gold Flake" ,, in packets of 10 ...	19/9 ,,
Player's Navy Cut ,, in packets of 10 ...	19/9 ,,
Wills' "Three Castles" ,, in packets of 10 ...	23/9 ,,
Wills' "Capstan" Navy Cut Tobacco, in ¼ lb. tins ...	4/8 per lb.
Player's Navy Cut Tobacco, in ¼ lb. tins	4/8 ,,

Can supply at above rates to Prisoners of War Associations which have H.M. Customs Bond Stores: cigarettes in cases of 50,000, tobacco in cases of 100 lbs.

Hand your order to any tobacconist, or mail direct to—

THE BRITISH-AMERICAN TOBACCO COMPANY, LTD.,
Ex. (Expeditionary) Department,
No. 7, Millbank, London, S.W.1.

BACON
❖ SPECIALLY CURED ❖
& PACKED IN CARTONS
❖ IN ½ & 1 lb. SIZES. ❖
Equally delicious
Boiled or Fried.

ROSE & ROSE
53, HAYMARKET. S.W.1
Telephones
Office...Gerrard 6277
Works...Streatham 1860
ORDER THROUGH THE
CENTRAL COMMITTEE

OXFORD'S
PATENT
PARCHMENT-COATED SUET
PUDDINGS
LIKE HOME MADE, BUT
WITHOUT TIN OR BASIN.
Lemon, Ginger,
Jam, Marmalade,
Raisin, Currant,
& other Varieties.

OXFORD'S LTD ...
... BURTON-ON-TRENT,
& 53, HAYMARKET, LONDON, S.W.1.
Order Through the Central Committee.

GWI-HF_62 The front cover of the monthly journal of the Central Prisoners of War Committee of the British Red Cross and Order of St. John. Providing goods for PoWs was big business.

GWI-HF_63 Three pictures showing the relatively relaxing life of a PoW in Britain.

GWI-HF_64 Newly-captured German sailors from the ten armed trawlers sunk during a sweep of the Cattegat on 15 April.

GWI-HF_65 'In memory of those who have fallen: the Bishop of London is blessing the war-shrine in Hyde Park.'

GWI-HF_66 As in Britain, money was raised in Germany to help those disabled by the war: the Ludendorff-Spende.

GWI-HF_67 Money was raised throughout the war to provide ambulances. This one was bought by the Scottish branch of the British Red Cross Society.

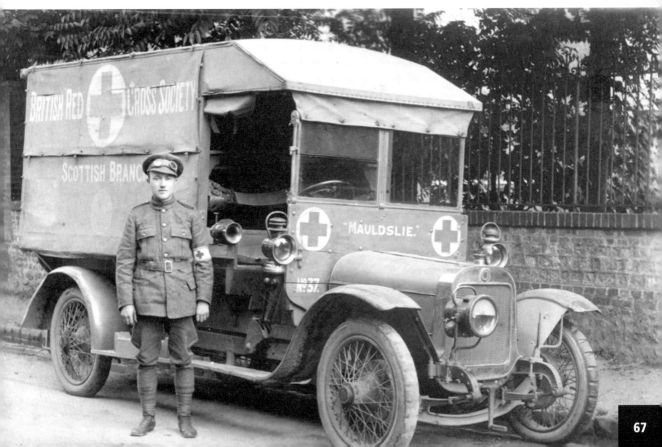

GWI-HF_69 Men unfit for further service were assisted in many ways. These ex-servicemen were being trained on Crown Colonies. After a period of training and assessment, those classed as proficient were allotted a cottage with 10 acres of land. This photo was taken at the 10,000-acre colony at Holbeach in Lincolnshire.

GWI-HF_68 Assistance was also provided to Britain's Allies, in this case France. This ambulance car, No. 100, was provided by the French Relief Fund.

GWI-HF_70 A one-armed man feeding the chickens at Holbeach Crown Colony.

GWI-HF_71 The winner in a competition to design a memorial plaque to commemorate those who fell in the war was Mr. E. Carter-Preston. He was awarded £250 for the design.

GWI-HF_72 Many of those killed on the Zeebrugge raid were buried in Britain, some in a mass grave at Dover, others in their home towns. This is the funeral of Royal Marine Private Gatehouse in Earley churchyard.

GWI-HF_73 The funeral of two officers and sixty-four men who fell in the naval raid on Zeebrugge and Ostend.

GWI-HF_74 The telegrams kept arriving, even though there was no fighting. Nominally safe in India, Private Hemmings succumbed to influenza two days after the signing of the Armistice.

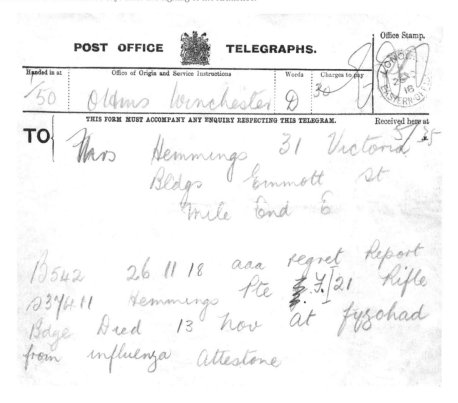

GWI-HF_75 Having survived the whole of the war, Private Mann of the 'Hull Pals' died of pneumonia on 14 November at home while recovering from wounds.

GWI-HF_76 A memorial card for 236312 Corporal Alfred Rayner who was killed in action on 29 August while serving with the 1st/8th West Yorkshire Regiment. His body was never found and he is commemorated on the Vis-en-Artois Memorial. He was a resident of Scarborough.

GWI-HF_77 The death columns in the glossy magazines generally contained photos of men; Mrs Margaret Gibson MM, administrator of QMAAC, was an exception. She was the first WAAC to receive the MM, awarded for conspicuous gallantry and devotion to duty during an air raid in Abbeville. She died of dysentery and is buried in Mont Huon Cemetery at Le Treport.

LIEUT.-COL. D. K. ANDER-
SON, M.C.,
(The Buffs) Machine-Gun Corps.
Mentioned in despatches.
Killed in action

LIEUT. COL. C. STRANGWAYS
LINTON, D.S.O., M.C.,
Worcester Regt. Son of late Mr.
H. P. Linton, and of Mrs. Linton,
Llandaff.

MAJ. J. G. ARCH-
DALE PORTER,
D.S.O.,
Lancers. Eldest son
of Mr. and Mrs.
Porter - Porter, of
Lisbellaw, Ireland.

GWI-HF_78 A more representative set of photographs from *The Illustrated London News*: five male officers who died in the line of duty. Bottom left is Major J. B. Macmillan, D.S.O., Duke of Cornwall's Light Infantry. A native of Culpar Fife he was killed in action. Bottom right is Staff Captain W. Alan-Fraser, M.I.D., (D.A.Q.M.G) of the Royal Engineers. He was killed in action.

GWI-HF_79 A rather unusual memorial card. This was for Private Robert Green, the dearly-beloved son of Robert and Mary Green of 9, Old Row, Success. He died of gunshot wounds on 5 October while serving with the 2nd South Staffordshire Regiment although his cap badge is the Durham Light Infantry.

In Loving Memory

GWI-HF_80 Another female who appeared in *The Illustrated London News* Roll of Honour was Nurse E.D. Pepper who died on 7 April and is buried in Cairo Military Cemetery.

Zum frommen Andenken im Gebete

an den tugendsamen Jüngling

Johann Geigl
Kölblbauernsohn von Leobendorf,
Gefrt. beim 1. bayr. Inf.-Regt., 3. Komp.,
Inhaber des Eisernen Kreuzes und des
Verdienstkreuzes mit Schwertern,

welcher nach 42 monatlicher, treuer Pflicht-
erfüllung am 21. August 1918 durch Brust-
schuß, im Alter von 23 Jahren den
Heldentod fürs Vaterland starb.

Er starb den Tod auf heißerkämpften Auen,
Fürs hart bedrängte Vaterland.
Nie werden wir ihm mehr ins Auge schauen
Und ihm nicht drücken mehr die Hand.
Er wird uns fehlen wenn die Brüder wiederkehren,
Nach hartem Kampf — zurück ins Vaterhaus.
Und unser Schmerz wird doppelt sich vermehren,
Vergeblich schaut das Auge nach ihm aus. —

O Herr gib ihm und allen gefallenen
Kriegern die ewige Ruhe!

Druck von Fritz Keerl, Laufen.

GWI-HF_81 Mrs V. Long of the QMAAC was drowned on the transport HMAT *Warilda*, a hospital ship bringing wounded from Le Havre. The ship was torpedoed on 3 August. Mrs Burleigh, who co-founded the QMAAC, was one of the 123 people lost in the sinking.

GWI-HF_82 Johann Siegl, a sergeant in 1 Bavarian Infantry Regiment, who died on 21 August after forty-two months' service.

Zum Andenken im Gebete

an

Franz Joseph Riester

Grenadier im Ref.-Jnft.-Regt. Nr. 64, 6. Komp.,

geboren den 1. April 1898 in Jungingen (Hohen=
zollern), gefallen den 23. August 1918 auf dem
Felde der Ehre bei Wangerie und wurde auf
dem Friedhof daselbst beerdigt.

GWI-HF_84 Johann Wintermayr was a farmer's son. He was killed in action in France on 18 September while serving with a trench mortar company. He had been awarded the Iron Cross 2nd Class and the Military Service Cross with swords.

Ich habe den guten Kampf gekämpft,
den Lauf vollendet, den Glauben
bewahrt.   II. Tim. IV., 7, 8.

GWI-HF_85 High School graduate Eugen Hartinger was a trainee officer when he was killed in action on 16 July. He was in charge of machine guns in Bavarian Infantry Regiment No. 19.

GWI-HF_86 Leutnant Hans Röhrner, winner of the Iron Cross and Military Service Cross, died in a hospital in Chowel (Kovel in Ukraine) on 17 December.

GWI-HF_87 A famous casualty of the flu epidemic was Captain Leefe Robinson VC. After repatriation from Germany in December 1918, he contracted the virus and died on the 31st.

Section 4

Food and Money

GWI-HF_88 The 'Feed the Guns' week in Trafalgar Square, was opened on 7 October by the Bishop of Kensington, seen here addressing the crowd.

GWI-HF_89 A novel way to help raise funds was the use of an airship to drop leaflets in March in connection with Business Men's Week.

GWI-HF_90 The gondola of an airship was detached and stationed in Trafalgar Square near the tank during Business Men's Week, 4-9 March. Each investor at the tank received a souvenir leaflet from the gondola.

GWI-HF_91 Sir Eric Geddes, First Lord of the Admiralty, is seen making a purchase of War Bonds at the gondola during Business Men's Week.

GWI-HF_92 Interested watchers of a leaflet falling from the airship during Business Men's Week.

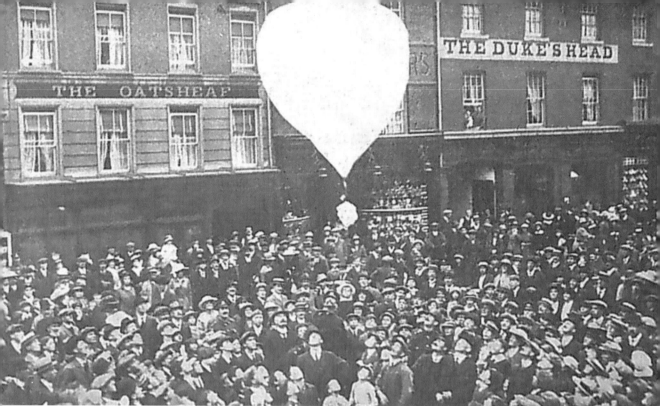

GWI-HF_93 A similar principle was used in Reading. A balloon was used to drop leaflets encouraging people to buy bonds.

GWI-HF_94 This YMCA flag was sold to raise money to provide huts for soldiers passing through London, and for huts abroad.

GWI-HF_95 Every nation at war sold bonds and each had its own style. This is a Canadian poster for Victory Bonds.

GWI-HF_96 There were many ways of collecting money. One was simply to ask for it. This is Countess Mazzuchi collecting money for the Red Cross in a large American flag. She was later accused of fraud.

GWI-HF_97 Two women in a wagon collecting money in support of the Committee for Free Milk for France, in New York City; whether this meant that they would send milk to France or pay for it in France was unclear.

GWI-HF_98 A dazzle-painted float (merchant ship) in the 4 July parade on Fifth Avenue.

GWI-HF_99 Showing the unity of the allied nations, British Royal Marines marched in the Liberty Loan procession through New York on 1 October 1918.

GWI-HF_100 To help raise money for the war effort, opera singer Geraldine Farrar sang in front of the New York Public Library. She was a member of the Women's War Relief Association.

GWI-HF_103 As well as an airship in Business Men's Week, the fountain basins in Trafalgar Square were used for a miniature fleet of warships.

Wrecked Building with Church Army Club in cellar.
(Note Church Army small shield at entrance.)

THE CHURCH ARMY:

(Registered under the War Charities Act 1916)

Its Losses in the Series of Battles which began on 21st March, 1918.

THE CHURCH ARMY is frequently asked, "What have been your exact losses since the beginning of the great enemy attack on 21st March?"

To the time of writing (the beginning of May, 1918), the Church Army has lost by enemy action about

100 RECREATION HUTS,

TENTS, CLUBS, established in buildings and similar centres; about one-half of the losses being in the area affected by the push towards Amiens, and the remainder in the battle area farther north. This figure is not an exact one. On the one hand, it is likely that a certain number of Huts, etc., will be reoccupied after being abandoned, and it is possible, on the other hand, that more will be lost before these pages are in print. That, however, is the position at the moment.

Each Hut represents an average expenditure of £500; each Tent, £300; and each other Centre a considerable sum spent on equipment and stores. The direct pecuniary loss to the Church Army is therefore great. More serious is the loss, just when most needed, of the help and comfort afforded by these institutions to our gallant men.

Fortunately, the gain to the enemy is small compared with our loss. In many cases, before a Hut was abandoned, our own troops were permitted to help themselves to the consumable stores, and the Hut itself was destroyed; and many, if not most of them, were in any case too severely knocked about to be of any use to the enemy. Some of the abandoned Huts have not passed into the enemy's hands at all, but have had to be evacuated on account

GWI-HF_101 The Church Army Hut Fund provided a safe house for soldiers near the front and on their way home. During the March offensive it had lost 100 huts in France. By May, it urgently needed funds. This leaflet was aimed to raise money to replace the losses.

GWI-HF_102 Onlookers watch as Trafalgar Square is prepared for the 'Feed the Guns Week' at the beginning of October.

GWI-HF_104 The preparations for the 'Feed the Guns Week' included the recreation of a Flanders landscape.

GWI-HF_105 Using a tank guaranteed a crowd. There were no tanks available in Australia so a dummy one was produced for Tank Week in Sydney. Here Sir Walter Davidson is seen opening the campaign in front of the Bank of Australia.

GWI-HF_106 Tank 130, known as *Nelson*, toured Britain with other tanks to raise funds.

To dear Ashton
With every appreciation of the
great help he gave us during Tank Week.

With all good wishes
Corporal Billy Brandon
Tank 130   Hull
11 Jan 1918

GWI-HF_108 Tank 130, *Nelson*, visited Hull in January and helped raise £2,186,820 in War Bonds.

York Tank Week.

Bank at the Tank in the Market Place and help to.

BUY MORE AIRSHIPS.

Britain's word is **HER** Bond and that Bond will win the War. Get **YOURS** now!

Dropped from a
British Airship.

Printed by the Yorkshire Herald Company, York.

GWI-HF_109 For towns too small for a tank to warrant a visit, there was always the pretend tank. This is believed to be Tank Week in Blackpool.

GWI-HF_107 A copy of the leaflet dropped by airship to help raise funds during Tank Week.

GWI-HF_110 Although India was a very large country there were no tanks available to use for Tank Week so a mock-up was made. This was taken in Calcutta during a war loan campaign.

GWI-HF_111 Germany also raised money through war loans. Even though there was money available, there was little interest in the ninth loan, pictured here in a propaganda photograph.

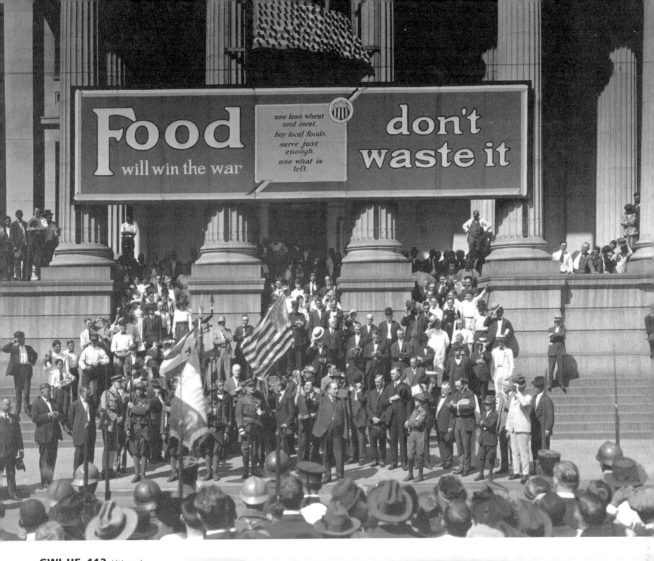

Food will win the war *use less wheat and meat. buy local foods. serve just enough. use what is left.* **don't waste it**

GWI-HF_112 Although America was a wealthy country with no shortage of food, the demands of war meant it had to reduce consumption like the other combatant nations.

GWI-HF_113 This is the Long Island Victory Special, organised by the women of the Long Island Food Reserve Battalion.

VICTORY SPECIAL = FOOD = DEMONSTRATION CAR

GWI-HF_114 Hamster adventures – city dwellers visiting the countryside to buy food were called hamsters. To help supplement the meagre rations, better-off Germans visited the countryside at weekends to try and buy food illegally. This postcard clearly shows how bad the food shortage had become in 1918 when no farmer was willing to sell any surplus food they had because of the possible punishment that could ensue. In most cases there was little to sell.

GWI-HF_115 To help the food shortage in Germany, the Red Cross ran food kitchens where a meal could be bought for 10 Pfennigs.

GWI-HF_116 An alternative to Red Cross meals was the Soup Cart.

GWI-HF_117 In order to control foodstuffs, municipal depots were set up. This one for potatoes is in Berlin.

GWI-HF_118 A 1918 postcard sent from the front to a family at home asking for supplies: 'Man does not live by bread alone, there must also be sausage and ham' and, added by the soldier who sent the card, 'and cigarettes'. Tobacco was in very short supply and was a valuable commodity on the Home Front and at the front.

GWI-HF_119 As the food shortages got worse, it became obvious that some form of rationing was necessary. On 26 January, civilians in Manchester demonstrated in favour of compulsory rationing.

GWI-HF_120 Food rationing required a lot of paperwork. Here workers are seen preparing food cards in Camberwell.

GWI-HF_121 This hive of activity is the Food Controller's registration headquarters at the Imperial Institute in London.

GWI-HF_122 Men on leave had to apply for emergency ration cards as they were not included in the initial distribution. Again this is the scene at Camberwell with men on leave applying for ration cards so they could eat.

RATIONING ORDER, 1918.

Instructions for the use of the New Ration Card. (N.86.)

1. During the autumn and winter you will require a Ration Card in place of the present Ration Book.

2. If any member of your household does not receive his Ration Card (by the time when re-registration begins in your district) he should make enquiries at the Food Office.

3. If any Card is sent to your house which you cannot deliver to the owner, send it back at once to your Food Office with a note explaining why it cannot be delivered.

4. See that your name and address and the name of your Local Food Office are correctly entered in the spaces at the top of your Card. If there is any mistake, ask the Food Office to correct it.

5. You will be required to register afresh, by means of the counterfoils on the Ration Card, for Meat, Butter and Sugar, with the retailers you choose. Unless you do this you will not be able to get proper supplies of these foods during the winter.

6. Your Food Office will announce, publicly, the week during which you must register, and any retailer will be able to tell you.

7. To register, write your name and address on the counterfoils A (Meat), B (Butter), and C (Sugar) on the lower part of the Ration Card, and give them to the retailers you choose.

8. See that your retailers stamp or write their names and addresses on the spaces A, B and C on the top of your Card, and also on the right hand side of the counterfoils.

9. The Food Office will require a short interval to ascertain the supplies which retailers will require for the customers who have registered with them by means of this Card. The new registration will, there-fore, not come into force till Monday, October 13th, 1919 : until this date you must continue to deal with the retailers with whom you are at present registered. After that date, you will, normally, unless you are the holder of an Emergency Ration Document, be able to obtain supplies of rationed food only from the retailers with whom you have registered by means of the counterfoils from the Ration Card.

10. The spare spaces D, E, and F, at the top of the Card, and the spare counterfoil, D, are for use in case other foods are rationed. Keep these spaces and the spare counterfoil blank until you receive instructions how to use them. Till then do not detach the spare counterfoil.

11. **The top portion of the Card will take the place of the Ration Book. You must keep it carefully. You must produce it to your Retailer if he asks you to do so.**

12. Supplies may be drawn only from the retailers whose names appear at the top of the Card and only so long as the holder of the Card is living in Great Britain, is not drawing Government Rations, is not staying in an hotel or boarding house, or is not living in an Institution (hospital, asylum, workhouse, etc).

13. If you are the person making purchases on behalf of the household you will either at the time when you give your retailers the counterfoils of the household, or at any time before October 13th, receive from each of the retailers with whom the household is registered a " Purchaser's Shopping Card." Each retailer must write or stamp his name and address on the Card and will enter on it the number of persons in the household who are registered with him for the food or foods in question. You must write your name and address on each card and must produce it to the retailer who issued it to you when making purchases from him. The cards will have spaces, one for each week, to be marked by the retailer when you make purchases. There will be two forms of Shopping Cards. One with spaces for meat which you will receive from the butcher, and one with spaces for butter and sugar. If you are registered with different retailers for butter and sugar you will receive a card from each, and each retailer must cross out the set of spaces which do not apply to him.

14. The " Purchaser's Shopping Card" will be valid only for purchases from the retailer whose name and address is on it. A Card which bears no retailer's name and address is not valid. The card will be valid only in respect of the members in each household registered with the retailer at the time of each purchase, and only for a food for which they are registered with him. When a household removes and changes its retailers it will get new cards from the new retailers.

15. If any member of a household removes or registers with another retailer since the Shopping Card has been issued to you, you must inform the retailer so that the number of persons stated on the card as being registered with him is altered. It will be an offence to make purchases on the card in respect of such members of the household.

16. **PERSONS ENTERING INSTITUTIONS.**—If the holder of a Ration Card enters an Institution, the Ration Card must be given up to the head of the Institution.

GWI-HF_123 A leaflet providing the instructions for the use of the ration card.

MINISTRY OF FOOD. Rationing Order, 1918.

(These instructions are additional to those printed in the Ration Book itself.)

1. If any book is sent to your house which you cannot deliver to its owner, send it back at once to your Food Office with a note explaining why it cannot be delivered.

2. Read the instructions on the cover of your ration book carefully, and in accordance with them :—
   (*a*) Sign your name and write your address on the cover of the book, on the reference leaf and on each page of coupons.
   (*b*) Take your book at once to each retailer with whom you are already registered and get him to enter his name and address in the proper space on the back of the cover. You must not change your retailer without the written consent of the Food Office.

3. JAM. You must register before November 10th with a retailer for jam. To do this you must fill up the Spare Counterfoil (iv.) leaf 5 (red). The retailer will enter his name and address on the proper space (No. 7) on the back cover and will detach and keep the counterfoil.

   Jam, marmalade, syrup, treacle, and honey will be rationed as from November 3rd, on the red coupons on leaf 5 marked "spare." You can buy jam and marmalade on these coupons only from the retailer with whom you are registered. You can buy syrup, treacle and honey on these coupons from any retailer who can supply you.

   Persons who will be between the ages of 6 and 18 at midnight on the 31st December next can obtain a supplementary ration of jam. These persons will receive a book containing an extra leaf of red coupons (Leaf 5x) with a counterfoil marked "Jam counterfoil" (supplementary). They must register this counterfoil, as well as the spare counterfoil (iv.), leaf 5, with a jam retailer.

INSTRUCTIONS IN CASE OF REMOVALS.

4. Always take your Ration Book with you if you go to stay away from home.

   If you have deposited any leaves of coupons with retailers, collect them before you start your journey.

   If you are removing permanently (*see paragraph 6*), you must, before starting, collect the counterfoils which you gave up from your old ration book when you registered with your retailers. If the retailer informs you that they are at the Food Office, you need not collect them but must tell the Food Office of the district to which you are moving.

TEMPORARY REMOVALS.

5. If you are going to stay in a hotel, boarding house, canteen, etc., you can use your ration book there without any formalities.

   If you are going to stay in a private house or lodgings, you will be able, so far as

3477. Wt. /F526. 6,000,000(*96*). 8/18 S.O.,F.Rd.

MINISTRY OF FOOD.

NATIONAL RATION BOOK (B).

INSTRUCTIONS.

Read carefully these instructions and the leaflet which will be sent you with this Book.

1. The person named on the reference leaf as the holder of this ration book must write his name and address in the space below, and must write his name and address, and the serial number (printed upside down on the back cover), in the space provided to the left of each page of coupons.

Food Office of Issue **LAMBETH**   Date 15/10/18

Signature of Holder *Barham Winifred M.L.*

Address *18 Romola Rd. Herne Hill S.E. 24*

2. For convenience of writing at the Food Office the Reference Leaf has been put opposite the back cover, and has purposely been printed upside down. It should be carefully examined. If there is any mistake in the entries on the Reference Leaf, the Food Office should be asked to correct it.

3. The holder must register this book at once by getting his retailers for butcher's meat, bacon, butter and margarine, sugar and tea respectively, to write their names and the addresses of their shops in the proper space on the back of the cover. Persons staying in hotels, boarding houses, hostels, schools, and similar establishments should not register their books until they leave the establishment.

4. The ration book may be used only by or on behalf of the holder, to buy rationed food for him, or members of the same household, or guests sharing common meals. It may not be used to buy rationed food for any other persons.

Continued on next page.

N. 2 J (Nov.)

IF FOUND, RETURN TO ANY FOOD OFFICE.

GWI-HF_124 Rationing was not a simple business. A further sheet of instructions for the use of a ration book.

GWI-HF_125 The front of a ration book issued to Winifred Barkham on 15 October.

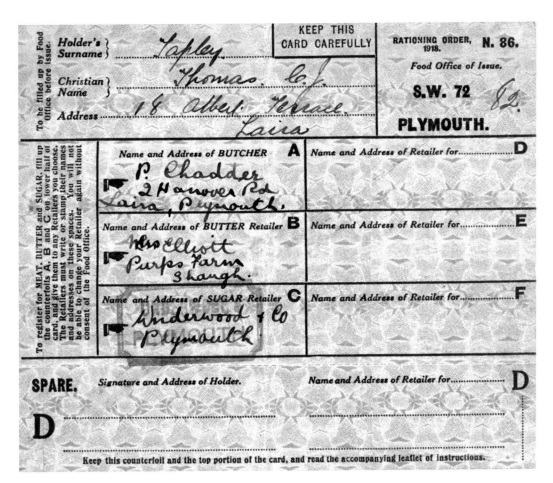

KEEP THIS CARD CAREFULLY

To be filled up by Food Office before issue.

Holder's Surname } *Tapley*

Christian Name } *Thomas. C.J.*

Address *18 Albert Terrace Laira*

RATIONING ORDER, 1918. **N. 86.**

Food Office of Issue.

S.W. 72 *82.*

PLYMOUTH.

To register for MEAT, BUTTER and SUGAR, fill up the counterfoils A, B and C on lower half of card, and give them to any Retailers you choose. The Retailers must write or stamp their names and addresses on these spaces. You will not be able to change your Retailer again without consent of the Food Office.

Name and Address of BUTCHER **A**
P. Chadder 2 Hanover Rd. Laira, Plymouth.

Name and Address of Retailer for............. **D**

Name and Address of BUTTER Retailer **B**
Mrs Elliott Purps Farm Shaugh.

Name and Address of Retailer for............. **E**

Name and Address of SUGAR Retailer **C**
Underwood & Co Plymouth

Name and Address of Retailer for............. **F**

SPARE.

D

Signature and Address of Holder.

Name and Address of Retailer for.............. **D**

Keep this counterfoil and the top portion of the card, and read the accompanying leaflet of Instructions.

GWI-HF_126 The inside of a ration book detailed the retailer who would provide the foodstuff.

L 17 **FOOD CARD.** **D. 3.**
London and Home Counties.

Customer's Name *Barham Ernest W.*

Address *18 Romola Rd. Herne Hill*

A. BUTTER AND MARGARINE.	1	2	3	4	5	6	7	8	9	10
	11	12	13	14	15	16	17	18	19	20

B.	1	2	3	4	5	6	7	8	9	10
	11	12	13	14	15	16	17	18	19	20

C.	1	2	3	4	5	6	7	8	9	10
	11	12	13	14	15	16	17	18	19	20

D.	1	2	3	4	5	6	7	8	9	10
	11	12	13	14	15	16	17	18	19	20

CUSTOMER'S PART.

D.
Shopkeeper's Name:

Address:

C.
Shopkeeper's Name:

Address:

GWI-HF_127 A London and Home Counties food card for butter and margarine.

GWI-HF_128 Food hoarding was a punishable offence. This commandeered supply of margarine is being given to a dairy to distribute.

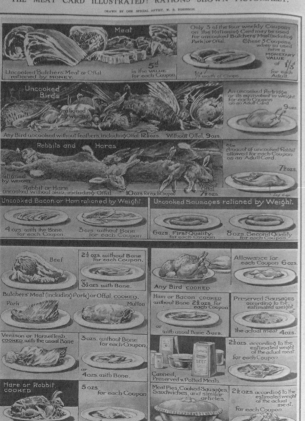

GWI-HF_129 The same was true of shops that had too much. It was distributed to other stores.

GWI-HF_130 A pictorial representation of the meat rationing situation in Britain.

	BRITAIN	GERMANY	AUSTRIA
BREAD	NOT RATIONED	3 lbs. 13¼ ozs.	2 lbs. 2 ozs.
MEAT	16 ozs.	7 ozs.	4·6 ozs.
FISH	NOT RATIONED	·87 oz.	NOT OBTAINABLE
MILK	NOT RATIONED	1½ PINTS.	·58 PINT
EGGS	NOT RATIONED	·25 EGG	NOT OBTAINABLE
BUTTER	4 ozs.	1·05 ozs. (?)	1 oz.
SUGAR	8 ozs.	8 ozs.	3½ ozs.
CEREALS:	NOT RATIONED	2·19 ozs.	1·4 ozs.
CHEESE.	NOT RATIONED	1·09 ozs.	¾ oz.
JAM	NOT RATIONED	3½ ozs.	2·4 ozs.
SYRUP.	NOT RATIONED	·87 oz.	·58 oz.
FRUIT	NOT RATIONED	NOT OBTAINABLE	11·7 ozs.
TEA	NOT RATIONED	SUBSTITUTE 1·75 ozs	SUBSTITUTE 1·1 ozs
COFFEE.	NOT RATIONED	SUBSTITUTE 2·19 ozs	SUBSTITUTE 1·4 ozs.
COCOA	NOT RATIONED	NOT OBTAINABLE	NOT OBTAINABLE
POTATOES.	NOT RATIONED	6 lbs.	7 lbs.
VEGETABLES.	NOT RATIONED	5 to 10 lbs	2 lbs 12 ozs

GWI-HF_131 Britain fared far better than the Central Powers for every foodstuff, as this chart clearly shows.

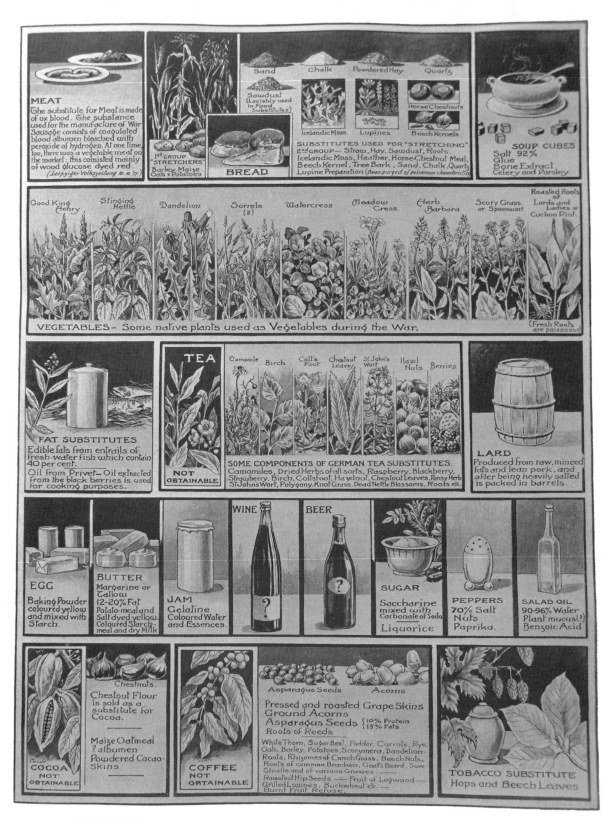

GWI-HF_132 German ingenuity replaced many foodstuffs with easily available alternatives, although not all of them were liked or were real substitutes. This chart shows just some of the ersatz products used.

Section 5

Women at War

GWI-HF_133 In Russia women were allowed to fight. This is Maria Leontievna Bochkareva who formed the Women's Battalion of Death and fought at the front. She visited the United States in 1918.

GWI-HF_134 By 1918 there were few jobs not done by women. This is rather low-level employment – painting the interior of a tank.

GWI-HF_135 This shows women employees at Kew Gardens, previously a male-dominated workforce.

GWI-HF_136 The German economy also used thousands of women in munitions but to a lesser extent than in Britain. These are German women making seaplane floats.

GWI-HF_137 A female employee of the Navy and Army Canteen Board, which ran canteens for servicemen in Britain.

GWI-HF_138 The numbers this munitionette is wearing are from fuse boxes. Perhaps she was encapsulating her employment in the fuse section in a clever way?

GWI-HF_140 The caption for this photograph was 'Aircraft work for women: welding wireless aerials.'

GWI-HF_139 As in the other combatant nations, women soon took the place of men who were called to the colours. Here women of the Woman's Reserve Camouflage Corps of the National League for Woman's Service are painting the Times Square War Savings Stamp theatre.

GWI-HF_141 The King and Queen are seen reviewing members of Queen Mary's Army Auxiliary Corps.

GWI-HF_142 Unlike Britain, America was quick to use women for police work. This is Captain Edyth Totten with new members of the Women's Police Reserve in New York City.

GWI-HF_144 There was no less dirt on the streets because there was a war on. Here women in Kingston are working as road-sweepers.

GWI-HF_143 With the shortage of food, it was essential to increase production. Thousands of women joined the Land Army to replace men called up.

GWI-HF_145 An organisation that thrived during the war was the Women's Volunteer Reserve. Mostly middle-class women, this group from Maidenhead assisted in hospitals.

GWI-HF_147 To help reduce the demand for flour, Mrs Weigall is seen here using potato as a flour substitute.

GWI-HF_148 Women police marching to Buckingham Palace on 6 July 1918. By the final year of the war they were a common sight.

GWI-HF_146 Women sewing covers on aeroplane wings was just one of the jobs performed in the aviation industry.

GWI-HF_149 Major General Sir Francis Lloyd, commanding the London District, is seen here inspecting the Women's Section of the Green Cross Motor Transport Reserve and men of the National Motor Transport Volunteers.

GWI-HF_150 This photograph served two purposes. Firstly it drew attention to the work being carried out by women, and secondly, it highlighted the need for more such women. As an incentive to undertake such work it noted that the pay was good and every employee was provided with a becoming outfit which included overalls, breeches, top-boots, and hat.

GWI-HF_151 A member of the Land Army wearing her brassard to show she is working for the war effort.

GWI-HF_152 The caption for this picture concerned class: society women at a Food Kitchen. 'The war is no respecter of persons, and has practically abolished differences of class.' The caption writer clearly thought this because Lady Cleveland, wife of Sir Charles Raitt Cleveland KCIE, was being served with a jug of soup at the Marylebone National Kitchen.

QUEEN MARY'S NEEDLEWORK GUILD.

BADGE CERTIFICATE.

Miss E. B. Terry

of _48 Combe Park, Bath_

having been engaged in voluntary war work for the Q.M.N.G. has been granted the badge of the Guild, which she is entitled to wear during the war, so long as she continues a voluntary worker.

St. James's Palace.

Annie Lawley
                    Hon. Sec.

Date _Sept. 16. 1918._

GWI-HF_154 At long last, work suitable for women: Queen Mary's Needlework Guild. It was formed on 21 August 1914 to help provide comforts for serving soldiers and sailors.

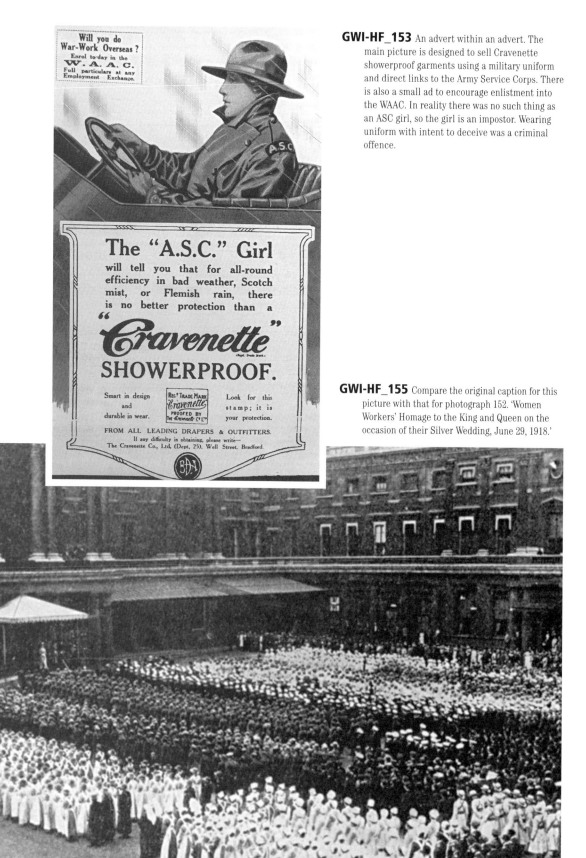

GWI-HF_153 An advert within an advert. The main picture is designed to sell Cravenette showerproof garments using a military uniform and direct links to the Army Service Corps. There is also a small ad to encourage enlistment into the WAAC. In reality there was no such thing as an ASC girl, so the girl is an impostor. Wearing uniform with intent to deceive was a criminal offence.

GWI-HF_155 Compare the original caption for this picture with that for photograph 152. 'Women Workers' Homage to the King and Queen on the occasion of their Silver Wedding, June 29, 1918.'

Section 6

Wartime life

GWI-HF_156 With the Russian exit from the war, a civil war broke out in Finland. Assisted by the Germans, the 'Whites' defeated the 'Reds'. With the German defeat in November, Finland became an independent, democratic republic. Here a German soldier is patrolling a railway bridge accompanied by a 'White' volunteer soldier. As the war was fought along the country's railways, the bridges were very important.

GWI-HF_157 A 'White' Guards rally in Helsinki.

GWI-HF_158 An unknown boy poses for a victory photograph.

GWI-HF_159 The government set up information bureaus, in large stores, railway stations and many other places, to provide the population with easy-to-read pamphlets about wartime life, especially about rationing and how to make food go further. This shows Lady Rhondda opening such a bureau.

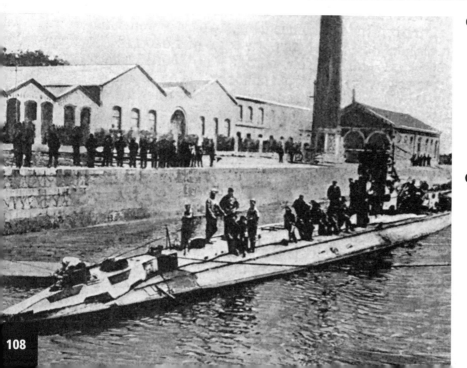

GWI-HF_160 The war touched neutral nations in a variety of ways. Spain lost a number of ships to U-boat attacks and in 1918 became the home for a badly-damaged German submarine. UC 48, commanded by Oberleutnant Lorenz, was depth-charged by HMS *Loyal* on 20 March 1918. The crew and vessel were interned at El Ferrol in Spain.

GWI-HF_161 Faith and Works: the Bishop of London at Stoke Newington in May 1918 dedicated two ambulances for service at the front.

GWI-HF_162 Somehow the Snowflake Laundry managed to get petrol for its pick-up and delivery truck – laundry could not have had a high priority. By 1918 many such vehicles had been converted to coal gas.

GWI-HF_163 A parade of private cars at Wellington Barracks. They had been placed at the public service by the National Motor Volunteers. In 1918 it had 433 vehicles available to assist as and when necessary.

GWI-HF_164 With a demand that was never satiated, the need for more and more shells required more and more workers. Naturally they were women. An advert for a further 120 workers at a shell factory near Oxford.

120 WOMEN URGENTLY WANTED

FOR

MUNITIONS WORK

In a NATIONAL FILLING FACTORY, near OXFORD.

STRONG BRITISH WOMEN—Age 18-45
Especially suitable.

No one already on Government work will be engaged.

GOOD WAGES.
Hostel and Lodging Accommodation Available.

Call at your Local Employment Exchange or fill in this form and post it **to-day** to the Employment Exchange, 29—31, London Street, Reading.

Please send me application form for Employment in National Filling Factory near Oxford.

Name ....

Address ....

GWI-HF_165 The demand for shipping increased with losses and naval expansion. American shipyards managed to streamline the manufacturing process and by mid-1918 could produce a destroyer in just seventy days. How long it took to work the ship up to handing over to the service was not indicated; possibly longer than the production time.

GWI-HF_167 A parade of more than 7,000 Special Constables was held in Regent's Park in May 1918. The purpose was to acknowledge the service provided by the men, all of whom had enrolled prior to January 1915 and served continuously since, by the award of a silver star.

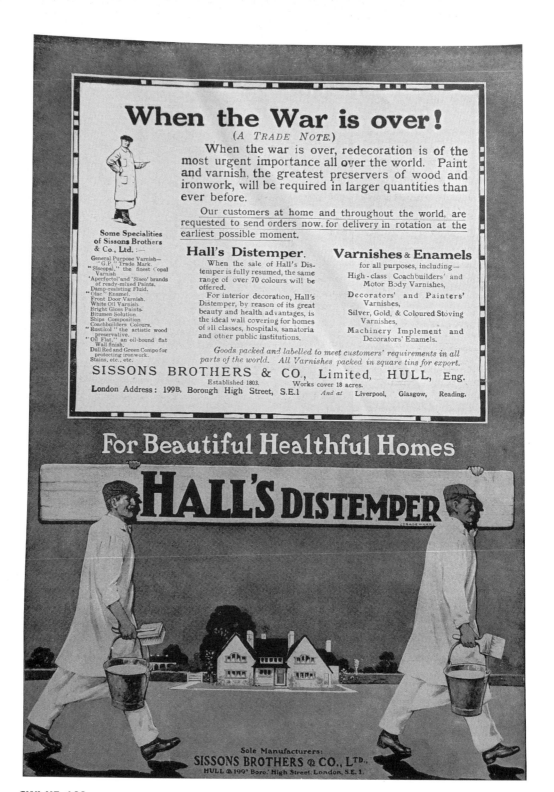

When the War is over!

(*A TRADE NOTE.*)

When the war is over, redecoration is of the most urgent importance all over the world. Paint and varnish, the greatest preservers of wood and ironwork, will be required in larger quantities than ever before.

Our customers at home and throughout the world, are requested to send orders now, for delivery in rotation at the earliest possible moment.

Some Specialities of Sissons Brothers & Co., Ltd. :—

General Purpose Varnish—"G.P." Trade Mark.
"Siscopal," the finest Copal Varnish
'Aperfectol' and 'Sisco' brands of ready-mixed Paints.
Damp-resisting Fluid.
"Olac" Enamel.
Front Door Varnish.
White Oil Varnish.
Bright Gloss Paints.
Bitumen Solution.
Ships Composition
Coachbuilders Colours.
"Rustikol" the artistic wood preservative.
"Oil Flat," an oil-bound flat Wall finish.
Dull Red and Green Compo for protecting ironwork.
Stains, etc., etc.

Hall's Distemper.

When the sale of Hall's Distemper is fully resumed, the same range of over 70 colours will be offered.

For interior decoration, Hall's Distemper, by reason of its great beauty and health advantages, is the ideal wall covering for homes of all classes, hospitals, sanatoria and other public institutions.

Varnishes & Enamels

for all purposes, including—

High-class Coachbuilders' and Motor Body Varnishes,

Decorators' and Painters' Varnishes,

Silver, Gold, & Coloured Stoving Varnishes,

Machinery Implement and Decorators' Enamels.

Goods packed and labelled to meet customers' requirements in all parts of the world. All Varnishes packed in square tins for export.

SISSONS BROTHERS & CO., Limited, HULL, Eng.

Established 1803.   Works cover 18 acres.

London Address: 199B, Borough High Street, S.E.1   *And at* Liverpool, Glasgow, Reading.

For Beautiful Healthful Homes

HALL'S DISTEMPER

Sole Manufacturers:
SISSONS BROTHERS & CO., LTD.,
HULL & 199ᵇ Boro.' High Street, London, S.E.1.

GWI-HF_166 Painting and decorating was deemed as secondary to the war effort. As a result public and private buildings were decidedly shabby by the end of the war. Anticipating the desire to restore the living environment to pre-war standards, a Hull company took out national adverts to promote its wares, even when it had little or none to sell.

GWI-HF_168 On a much smaller scale, a parade of Special Constables in Reading, commemorating their service.

GWI-HF_169 There were regular visits to foreign nations by ceremonial troops of the Allies. This is the visit of the Italian Carabinieri which landed at Folkestone and then entrained for London.

GWI-HF_170 The wine produced would be weak and acidic, but the harvest had to be collected. Collecting the grapes in the Pfalz area for the vintage of 1918.

GWI-HF_172 As the German Empire collapsed, revolution broke out in Germany. Revolutionary soldiers sleep while a sentry is on duty.

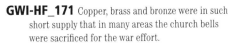
GWI-HF_171 Copper, brass and bronze were in such short supply that in many areas the church bells were sacrificed for the war effort.

GWI-HF_173 A street demonstration in Berlin by revolutionaries carrying a red flag.

FÊTE DE L'INDÉPENDANCE AMERICAINE A PARIS LE 4 JUILLET 1918 (4ᵉ Année de Guerre)
Le Défilé des Américains
AMERICAN INDEPENDENCE DAY IN PARIS, JULY 4ᵗʰ 1918 (4ᵗʰ Year of War)

GWI-HF_174 Regardless of the war, a parade was obligatory on American Independence Day. This one was in Paris.

GWI-HF_175 Paper was in short supply among the warring nations and its recycling became big business. Accompanied by the obligatory male, these women are collecting paper for pulping.

GWI-HF_177 In Bavaria, like in Britain, the ruling family celebrated a wedding anniversary. The difference was twenty-five years. King Ludwig III and Queen Maria Theresa were celebrating their golden wedding.

Ernemann Feld-Kameras

DIE BESTEN ERFOLGE AUF ALLEN KRIEGS-
SCHAUPLÄTZEN BEZUG DURCH ALLE PHOTO-
HANDLUNGEN PREISLISTE KOSTENFREI

Ernemann-Werke A.G. Dresden 120

PHOTO-KINO-WERKE   OPTISCHE ANSTALT.

GWI-HF_176 There is a definite irony, probably unintended, in this advert: there was a severe shortage of photographic supplies in Germany but regardless it encourages soldiers to take photos. It also contrasts with the Allied view of a totalitarian state: in Germany taking photographs at the front was allowed but in Britain, a free country, it was a court-martial offence.

GWI-HF_178 There was such a shortage of metal in Germany that even high denominations were replaced by paper notes produced by the town for use only in the town or city of production. This 10 Mark note was issued by the city of Kiel just before the mutiny.

Gutschein der Stadt Kiel
über
№ 732639
Zehn Mark
KIEL, DEN 15. OKTOBER 1918.

Oberbürgermeister Bürgermeister   Stadtverordn.-   Stellv. Stadtv.-
                                   Vorsteher   Vorsteher

South Berks Hunt.

HORSE FLESH TO FEED HOUNDS is badly wanted. Farmers and others would greatly help the Master by advising him of any flesh available. A fair price will be given. Knacker's cart sent at once. Phone 14 Pangbourne.

The Kennels, Purley, Reading.

GWI-HF_179 During the year, fox-hunting restarted. As the food situation was improving, there was less of a demand for horse flesh. The South Berks Hunt was happy to take any surplus horse-meat to feed their dogs.

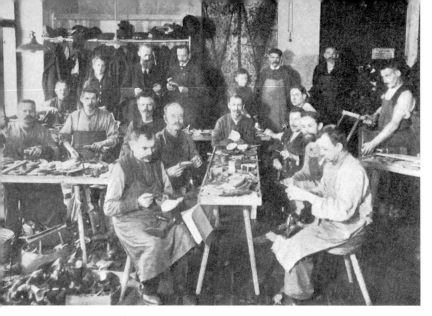

GWI-HF_180 In Britain careful control of leather meant that there was enough for civilian shoes while in Germany leather was a very scarce commodity. Here cobblers are mending soles with wood.

GWI-HF_181 Formamint could never be sold today with such claims: a mint that helped fend off the flu – not to be confused with so-called formalin tablets.

Why catch their Influenza?

YOU need not! Just carry Formamint with you and suck these delicious tablets whenever you are in danger of being infected by other people.

"Suck at least four or five a day" — so says Dr. Hopkirk in his standard work "Influenza" — for "in Formamint we possess the best means of preventing the infective processes which, if neglected, may lead to serious complications."

Seeing that such complications often lead to Pneumonia, Bronchitis, and other dangerous diseases, it is surely worth while to protect yourself by this safe, certain, and inexpensive means. Protect the children, too, for their delicate little organisms are very exposed to germ-attack. Be careful, however, not to confuse Formamint with so-called formalin tablets, but see that it bears the name of the sole manufacturers: Genatosan, Ltd. (British Purchasers of Sanatogen Co.), 12, Chenies Street, London, W.C. 1. (Chairman: The Viscountess Rhondda.)

"Attack the germs before they attack you!"

Though genuine Formamint is scarce your chemist can still obtain it for you at the pre-war price — 2/2 per bottle. Order it to-day.

Formamint
THE GERM KILLING THROAT TABLE

GWI-HF_182 At a village festival in Alsace, after their liberation, a veteran of the Franco-Prussian war poses with younger
members of the village who are wearing respirators left behind by the retreating German troops.

GWI-HF_183 A soldier is demonstrating a Browning automatic rifle outside the New York City library to a group of society women. The event was sponsored by the Mayor's Committee of Women on National Defense.

GWI-HF_184 Not a woman in sight in this German aircraft factory.

GWI-HF_185 In Germany such skilled work was for men: putting an aircraft together.

GWI-HF_186 As has been seen in previous books, the Royal Family maintained a high profile by regularly visiting factories and plants across the country. Here the Prince of Wales is seen visiting a factory on the Clyde.

GWI-HF_188 In June, the King and Queen visited an aircraft factory in Bedford.

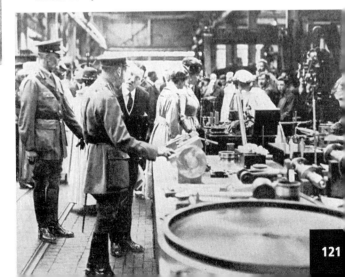

GWI-HF_187 On 23 March, the King and Queen paid an informal visit to a working men's club in Richmond. Here the Queen is seen being saluted by Girl Guides during the visit.

GWI-HF_189 On St. George's Day, Princess Alice served on a stall in Market Place, Windsor. The Queen, with Princess Mary, Prince Henry and Prince George, drove through the town and into the Market Place, to a sale of flowers and vegetables.

GWI-HF_190 American sailors saluting King George during his visit to their troopship, USS *Finland*, docked at Liverpool.

GWI-HF_191 'Girls of the Land Army at Buckingham Palace: Reviewed by her Majesty.' They were led, said the caption, 'by a handsome girl "divinely tall," picturesque in a long coat, knee-breeches, and leggings.'

GWI-HF_192 The King is seen here inspecting root-crop specimens at Suttons Seeds in Reading.

GWI-HF_193 On the third day of his Clyde tour, the Prince of Wales is watching a rotary plane machine in action.

GWI-HF_194 Throughout the war, King George invested many soldiers and sailors around the country. Here he is shaking hands with the son of a deceased soldier.

GWI-HF_195 The King is inspecting the seeds held by Suttons Seeds in Reading.

GWI-HF_196 Most medal investitures were held at Buckingham Palace. Here the King is awarding the VC to acting CSM John Skinner. On the bottom of his sleeve can be seen vertical metal bars, one for each wound, five in total.

GWI-HF_197 Such was the shortage of leather that these children are not wearing shoes on their way to school.

GWI-HF_199 The elephants at Berlin Zoo were made to earn their living during the winter of 1917/18. During a severe shortage of haulage trucks, they were made to pull loads around the city.

GWI-HF_200 With a shortage of labour in Germany, even the aristocracy had to get their hands dirty. Here a Count and his family are clearing snow from the roads in Berlin.

GWI-HF_198 Rubber was virtually unobtainable so new ways had to be invented to make travel in cars possible. One solution was a series of springs, seen here. It was functional rather than comfortable.

GWI-HF_201 It was a simple matter to make up for manpower shortages in some occupations. German children on their way to work: picking grapes in the autumn of 1918.

GWI-HF_203 Little had changed in Ireland during the war. The poor were still poor.

GWI-HF_204 Glass bottles were in short supply and commanded good prices when recycled. These Scouts are collecting to raise money for motor ambulances.

GWI-HF_202 German workers fitting the struts to a fighter plane.

GWI-HF_205 During the police strike there was no major crime wave as predicted. People went about their business lawfully as usual. Not all the police went on strike and there were of course thousands of Special Constables to assist.

GWI-HF_207 Part of the 4 July parade on 5th Avenue in New York City.

GWI-HF_206 There was considerable anti-German feeling in America. On 19 August, German-American farmer John Meints was whipped, tarred and feathered for not supporting war bond drives. The men involved were acquitted but in 1922 Meints won an appeal.

GWI-HF_208 Women dressed to represent the French Provinces of Alsace and Lorraine are marching along 5th Avenue as part of the 4th of July celebrations.

GWI-HF_209 These two servicemen are enjoying Thanksgiving, courtesy of the population of New York City which turned host and cared for every man in uniform.

GWI-HF_210 Another parade in New York City, this time for the Red Cross on 5 May.

GWI-HF_212 King George is taking the salute at a parade of sailors who have taken part in almost every naval engagement of the war.

GWI-HF_211 Another parade in New York City, this time in May for the Anzac soldiers passing through on their way to Europe. With such crowds it was also a good time to publicize the latest issue of Liberty Bonds.

GWI-HF_213 Parades provide focus and a positive feeling about achievements past and to come. This was the great rally of Boy Scouts and Girl Guides at Foot's Cray in Kent.

GWI-HF_214 It was not only German planes that could cause destruction. A plane from 37 TS (Training School) crashed on 23 March, injuring the two crew members: fortunately it did not hit the building.

GWI-HF_215 'On the news of the recovery of Lille, the Lillois living in Paris marched to the Place de la Concorde, removed the crepe which had been hung on the Statue of Lille since the German occupation of the city, and replaced that emblem of mourning with garlands and flags.'

GWI-HF_216 The population of Lille in the Grand Place, cheering the arrival of British troops on 17 October.

GWI-HF_217 Chinese officers visiting recently recaptured territory in Alsace on 4 August.

GWI-HF_218 American troops relaxing behind the lines in France.

GWI-HF_219 So many Americans arrived that they appeared to be everywhere. Sightseers in London during August.

GWI-HF_220 To increase understanding about – and increase participation in – the war, the British government staged war exhibitions across America. Naturally in the southern states the exhibitions were segregated. This picture was taken on a 'Coloured Day' when non-whites were allowed to view the exhibits.

GWI-HF_221 Although taking holidays was frowned upon during the latter part of the war, some people took no notice and went to the coast for a day or two, like this young lady on the beach somewhere on the south coast. The card was sent from Folkestone.

GWI-HF_222 With the shortage of petrol for the domestic market, the engines of many vehicles were altered to run on coal gas.

GWI-HF_223 Farmers too were affected by the shortage of fuel. To combat the shortage some tractors were converted to coal gas power.

GWI-HF_224 A view of HMS *Vindictive* in harbour at Dover after the Zeebrugge raid.

GWI-HF_225 On 3 March, three men of the Dover Patrol received medals for distinguished service: (left to right) Deckhand A. Holt, Engineer T.H. Walkerley, and Seaman A. Chambers.

GWI-HF_226 Some of the men of the Zeebrugge raid on their return to Dover.

GWI-HF_227 Little notice is being taken of the Germans as they evacuate Liège.

GWI-HF_228 German troops in the Place St. Lambert in Liège waiting for the order to leave.

GWI-HF_229 German troops passing through a Belgian village as they withdrew to the final defensive line.

GWI-HF_231 As the Germans retreated, the severity of the war on towns behind the lines became apparent. This is the Rue Émile Zola in Lens.

GWI-HF_232 The residents of Vouziers are shown here fleeing from French artillery fire.

GWI-HF_233 Arras had been bombarded since the start of the war and much of the city lay in ruins. This is the cathedral just after the war had ended.

GWI-HF_230 The VAD procession on 28 April in Sydney.

CAMBRAI APRÈS LA LIBÉRATION.
Un groupe de Maisons de la Grande Place.

GWI-HF_234 The Grande Place in Cambrai after its liberation. There was much work to be done to restore the city.

GWI-HF_235 As in the devastated cities and towns, so also there was much work to be done in the countryside. Villages needed to be rebuilt and battlefields cleared of debris, ordnance and the dead. This picture is of Mont Kemmel at the end of the war.

Ruines du Mont Kemmel
The ruins of Kemmel-Hill
1914-18

Au sommet du Mont. Un trou de mine et son contenu.

On the summit of the hill A shell hole and its contents.

Section 7

Armistice

GWI-HF_236 Mons was liberated on the last day of the war. Here the advancing troops are marching through the crowds.

GWI-HF_239 A street scene in Paris on Armistice Day.

GWI-HF_237 A clearer view of the triumphal entry of the Allied forces in Mons.

GWI-HF_238 Postcard makers were quick off the mark to cash in on popular sentiment.

GWI-HF_240 Rejoicing in Paris on Armistice Day at the Place de l'Opéra.

GWI-HF_241 Another scene of the celebrations in Paris on 11 November.

GWI-HF_242 Celebrating Armistice Day in Cambridge. An effigy of the Kaiser is being carried around the city.

GWI-HF_243 In Italy: these are the celebrations around the Garibaldi monument in Genoa.

GWI-HF_244 And in Japan: here Japanese schoolchildren are celebrating victory with a kite-flying display in Tokyo.

GWI-HF_245 Smaller than the celebrations in London but just as lively: the centre of Reading on Armistice Day.

GWI-HF_246 The crowds celebrating Armistice Day in Sydney.

GWI-HF_247 Connaught Place in Ottawa on 11 November. The armistice is being celebrated at the same time as a Victory Loan drive was proceeding with an open-air cinema, a sand-bag tea hut and captured guns.

GWI-HF_248 The crowds outside Buckingham Palace after news that the armistice had been signed.

GWI-HF_249 Crowds waiting outside 10 Downing Street for an appearance from Lloyd George on Armistice Day.

GWI-HF_250 Crowds at the entrance to the War Office on Armistice Day.

GWI-HF_251 The crowds outside Buckingham Palace waiting for the King to appear.

GWI-HF_252 Hospital workers driving through London celebrating the armistice.

GWI-HF_253 Flag-waving and cheering men and women crowding a motor bus.

GWI-HF_254 Celebrating Armistice Day with the help of a cartoon of the Kaiser.

GWI-HF_255 Flag-waving women of the WRAF seen in London on 11 November.

GWI-HF_257 As there were no restrictions on lighting in the evening, the Royal Navy lit up the sky in celebration.

GWI-HF_256 A new use for an 'All Clear' car and a car commandeered by the crowds.

GWI-HF_258 Very quickly after Armistice Day, PoWs began to be repatriated. Some of the first arrived in Hull on SS *Archangel* on 17 November.

OFFICERS & SOLDIERS IN UNIFORM.

GWI-HF_259 Not long after repatriation began, some lucky troops arrived in England for demobilisation; many had to wait months for release.

GWI-HF_260 The Americans rapidly began their demobilisation programme. This is the SS *Mauretania*, still in dazzle camouflage, taking American troops home.

GWI-HF_261 Some of the first Americans sent home were recovered wounded troops.

GWI-HF_262 A subdued welcome for returning American troops.

Section 8

Christmas

With the best of Good Wishes for Christmas and all time.

From the British Red Cross Society and Order of St. John. Xmas 1918.

GWI-HF_263 A final war-time Christmas card from the Red Cross.

GWI-HF_265 No snow to remind the men of Christmas in Mesopotamia, just sun, sand and flies.

GWI-HF_266 Greetings from the Salonika Army in Macedonia where the war had finished on 30 September.

155

Xmas Greetings from
the 7th. Division
19
Ita

Letters from Home

GWI-HF_264 As in previous years, Christmas cards came from all over the world, but this time with a difference, the men were waiting to be demobilised. This card is from the 7th Division serving in Italy.

GWI-HF_267 For the family at home, it would be the last Christmas card from their men serving half a world away.

No. 1 Australian
Auxiliary Hospital
Harefield, Middlesex

1915   1918

GWI-HF_268 The war might be over but in hospitals across the world there were still tens of thousands of wounded men. They were given as good a Christmas as possible.

1918 Home Front Timeline

January

1   Retail food prices (RFP) now 106 per cent compared to 1914. Sugar rationing provides 8oz per person a week. Local lard rationing provides 2oz a week per person.

3   Air Council established.

4   Hospital ship *Rewa* sunk in the Bristol Channel.

5   Lloyd George addresses TUC Manpower Conference on war aims; forms new cabinet.

8   In Lisbon a naval revolt is put down.

10 House of Lords adopts women's suffrage clause.

12 Workers loot closed food shops in Leytonstone and Wembley.

13 Due to German submarine activity, Norway rations coffee, corn and meal and sugar.

14 The House of Commons reassembles and Sir A. Geddes introduces Manpower Bill to provide the army with over 400,000 more men. Yarmouth bombarded by enemy destroyers – 6 killed and 6 injured. British bombers attack Karlsruhe in daylight raid. Ex-PM of France charged with treason; convicted on lesser charge in February 1920 but soon released.

15 Draft of compulsory rationing scheme issued to Control Committees.

16 A cut in the bread rations, 7 ½ to 6oz, and lack of progress on Eastern Front causes a general strike in Austria. Committee of enquiry into expenditure of government departments announced.

17 To combat German air raid threat, the London Air Defence area has nearly 100 operational fighters.

18 Austrian strike spreads to Hungary. A severe coal shortage in America results in no-war industry east of the Mississippi until 22 January.

21 Sir E. Carson resigns. Manpower Bill passes committee stage. Austrian general strike finishes.

23 Public meals order. Average daily cost of the war is now £7.5 million. Labour Party Conference meets in Nottingham and suggests an International Labour Peace Conference to be held in Switzerland.

24 Lord Rhondda outlines comprehensive scheme of national food distribution.

25 36th meeting of Irish Convention considers letter from the Prime Minister.

28 Aeroplane raid on Kent, Essex and London – 67 killed and 166 injured; one machine brought down. A peace strike of 400,000 in Berlin lasts until 4 February.

29 Aeroplane raid on Kent, Essex and the outskirts of London – ten killed and ten injured.

30 Air raid on Paris causes 259 casualties resulting in many Parisians wanting to move south. One Gotha brought down. Peace strikes spread across Germany.

31 Martial law declared in Berlin and Hamburg resulting in some factories becoming militarised and many workers drafted.

February

1 RFP now 108 per cent (in Turkey, 1,970 per cent). Bread ration cards introduced in Paris.

3 Berlin strikers told to return to work or be shot.

5 Bread riots in the Loire, France.

6 Electoral Reform Act passed giving 6 million women over 30 the vote. Home Army rations now at civilian level.

7 London Air Defence Area now has 200 aircraft, 323 searchlights and 249 AA guns. Saarbrücken attacked by French bombers.

10 Lord Beaverbrook appointed Minister in charge of propaganda.

11 Demonstration in Brussels over German plans to create a separate Flanders, splitting Belgium into two countries.

12 Theatres on Broadway closed to save coal. In France the sale or manufacture of confectionery is forbidden.

13 Pacifist group in House of Commons defeated.

15 Submarine shells Dover – one killed and seven injured. Trawler and seven drifters sunk in Straits of Dover.

16 Aeroplane raid on Kent, Essex and London – twelve killed and six injured, one machine brought down.

17 Aeroplane raid on Kent, Essex and London – twenty-one killed and thirty-two injured. Bolo Pasha executed.

19 Aeroplane raid on Kent, Essex and London; the aircraft failed to penetrate the London Defences.

20 Inter-Allied Labour and Socialist Conference meets at Westminster.

25 Austrians bomb Venice. Rationing of meat, butter and margarine comes into force in London and the Home Counties.

26 Lawlessness in Ireland; additional troops sent to aid the police. Venice bombed by Austrians.

March

1 RFP down 1 per cent to 107. Fat and butter rationing cards introduced in Switzerland.

3 Kaiser orders flags in every city and a day off from school to celebrate peace with Russia. In Turkey the Muslims of Samsun massacre Armenians.

4   Austrians bomb Venice for eight hours. 'Businessmen's week' sells £138m of national war bonds. Louise Smith sentenced to ten years for spying.
7   Aeroplane raid on Kent, Essex, Hertfordshire, Bedfordshire and London – twenty-three killed and thirty-nine injured; one Gotha downed. Vote of credit for £600 million; war now costing £6.75 million a day.
8   Paris air raid results in fifty-nine casualties.
9   British planes bomb Mainz. German airships bomb Naples.
10 British planes bomb Stuttgart Daimler factory. Exodus of 200,000 from Paris as result of bombing.
11 War Bond week produces £138,870,240. National Expenditure Committee report on extravagance in munitions.
12 Zeppelin raid on East Riding, Hull bombed – one dies of shock. Zeppelin raid on Durham, Hartlepool bombed – eight killed and thirty-nine injured.
15 A grenade explosion in a Courneuve factory totally destroys the area, kills 14, wounds 1500.
19 The House of Lords debates a resolution approving principle of League of Nations.
21 British miners under 25 lose military exemption.
24 British bombers attack Cologne.
26 Churchill asks factories for Easter holidays' deferment; not all comply. Heating and Power Order restricts lighting in public places after 10.30 pm.
28 Women's Auxiliary Army Corps formed by Army Council instruction; headed by Mrs Chalmers Watson. Anti-conscription riots in Quebec.
29 Long range German gun causes 165 civilian casualties in church of St. Gervais. French vote to call up the class of 1919. Due to the gravity of the war news, newspapers were published and sold on Good Friday.

April

1   Royal Air Force formed from RNAS and RFC. Women's RAF set up. RFP same as January. Troops fire on anti-conscription riots in Quebec.
5   In Collinsville, Illinois, German immigrant Robert Prager is lynched as a suspected spy; alleged perpetrators acquitted.
6   Third US Liberty Bond drive begins with aim of raising $3 billion.
7   Meat rationing extended to the whole of Britain.
9   Lloyd George introduces Manpower Bill which provides for comb-out of munitions workers, call-up of more miners, transport workers and civil servants. Military age raised to 50. French bread allowance cut.
10 Manpower Bill passed with a majority of 223, to have effect from 24 April.
11 Wastepaper collection at 1,100 tons a month. Food riots in Holland.

12   Military service for Ireland agreed by a majority of 165. Last Zeppelin raid on Britain–seven killed and twenty injured.

16   Final reading of the Manpower Service Bill, passed by a majority of 198.

18   Dublin Mansion House conference, after consultation with Bishops, denies right of British government to enforce conscription. The third Military Service Act becomes law, lowering age to 17½ and raising it to 50, and lessening eyesight requirements.

20   First National Emergency Proclamation, withdrawing exemptions up to 23¼ years. Nationalist MPs unanimously decide to oppose conscription; Irish bishops support them. Lord Derby replaced as War Minister.

22   Budget proposals – income tax to be raised to 6 shillings. Farmers' tax doubled. Two-penny cheque stamp. Beer and spirit duty doubled. Tobacco, match and sugar duty raised. Luxury tax introduced. Letter rate raised. Expenditure £972,197,000 and revenue £842,050,000, showing a deficit of £2,130,147,000.

23   Newfoundland introduces conscription. Guatemala declares war on Germany.

25   Red Cross sale produces £151,000. 750,000 women working in munitions.

26   Meatless days in France increased to three a week.

28   Assassin of Archduke Ferdinand, Gavrilo Princip, dies in hospital of tuberculosis.

29   Bonnet Rouge treason trial opens.

May

1   May Day strike at St. Étienne involves 35,000 armaments workers. First War Loan in Constantinople. Ludendorff Fund for War Wounded opens.

5   Meat ration reduced in Britain.

7   Manchester aircraft workers strike.

8   Nicaragua declares war on Austria and Germany.

11   The King reviews American troops in London.

12   German Navy invades St. Kilda and shoots sheep.

13   Over 40,000 French munition workers strike against the war.

14   Arrest of about 150 Sinn Fein leaders in Ireland for plotting with Germany. Denaturalization of Dangerous Aliens Bill issued. Over 100,000 French workers now on strike.

15   Air mail service between New York and Washington opens. At conclusion of Bonnet Rouge trial, editor Duval sentenced to death.

16   In Britain excess profits on food penalised.

17   British planes bomb Thionville and Metz-Sablon. In Britain all men born in 1898 or in 1899 are called up.

18   Third US Liberty Bond drive finishes having raised $4.1 billion. British bombing attack on Cologne kills 110. Metal workers strike in the Loire.

19   Largest, last and costliest bomber raid on Kent, Essex and London caused considerable damage – 49 killed and 177 injured; 5 raiders brought down.

22   Air raid on Paris causes twenty-three casualties.

24   Government issues statement exposing Sinn Fein intrigues with Germany and the revolutionary movement in Ireland. American hotels can hire black waiters due to shortage of white men.

25   Loire metalwork strikers' leaders arrested and seventy-three strikers drafted.

26   RN patrol yacht *Lorna* sinks *UB74* in Lyme Bay.

27   Air raid on Paris, one attacker lost.

28   Government opens discussions with Germany for direct exchange of prisoners on lines of Franco-German convention.

29   Report of Food Production Department shows that four million acres have been added for tillage and that 4/5ths of the country's food for the year will be home grown. Criminal 'Black Book' libel case opens at the Old Bailey.

31   British planes bomb Karlsruhe causing seventy-eight casualties. In Constantinople a great fire burns for twenty-seven hours.

June

1   Air raid on Paris causes twenty-eight casualties. Start of flu pandemic in Britain and India. RFP at February level. In France food rationing cards become compulsory. Manpower shortage for the army results in the call-up of the 1920 class in Germany. Inquiry into conscientious objectors authorised in America and 130 Mennonites jailed.

3   Lord French wants to reward Irish volunteer soldiers with land.

4   Majority of 18-year-old men in Britain lose their military service obligation exemption.

5   The second draft registration in America adds 750,000 21-year-olds to the army.

14   In Britain, men of 50 required to report as needed for the draft.

15   Committee of Ministers for Home Affairs formed under the chairmanship of Sir G. Cave. Aeroplane raid on Kent – no casualties. Vote of credit for £500 million. Lord Curzon announces abandonment of Home Rule and conscription in Ireland for the present.

17   In Britain men born 1895 to 1897 called up, excluding shale oil workers and shipbuilders. Strikes in Vienna over reduced bread ration.

20   For the duration of the war, women lift operators are to be allowed.

22   Rail crash in Tennessee kills ninety-nine and injures seventeen.

25   British bomb Karlsruhe.

26   Aircraft workers strike. British bomb Karlsruhe, Mannheim and Saarbrücken. Sugar rationing introduced in America, 3lbs a month per person.

29   French raise income tax to 30 per cent and customs duty and other indirect taxes. At Buckingham Palace the King addresses 2,540 uniformed women, paying tribute to their work.

July

1   Serious explosion at shell factory in Midlands – 134 killed and 150 injured. RFP now 110 per cent. Flu pandemic continues. National Baby Week in Britain to help lower rate of infant mortality.

3   Proclamation of Sinn Fein as dangerous organisation.

6   King George's Silver Wedding anniversary.

9   Appointment of J.R. Clynes MP as Food Controller.

11   Government announces stricter treatment of enemy aliens. Miners in Silesia strike, mines taken over by the military.

12   Denaturalisation Bill passes first and second readings in the House of Commons. Haiti declares war on Germany.

13   Protest in Trafalgar Square against aliens supposedly at large.

14   British yards produce their first all-welded steel ship.

15   British planes bomb Saarbrücken centre. In France the trial for treason of ex-Interior Minister Valpy begins.

17   Editor of Bonnet Rouge executed for receiving money from the Germans.

18   Aeroplane raid on Kent – no casualties.

19   Denaturalisation Bill passes third reading. Honduras declares war on Germany.

20   Aeroplane raid on Kent – no casualties. Threatening meeting of munitions workers in Birmingham.

21   Ministry of Munitions appeals to workers not to strike during critical battle.

22   Lord Lee resigns as Director of Food Production.

23   Munitions workers' strike at Coventry affects tank production. King visits the Grand Fleet.

24   Birmingham munitions workers go on strike.

21   Conference of National Engineering and Allied Trades' Council decide to strike if there is no settlement before 30 July.

22   Government issues an ultimatum to munitions workers: after 29 July, return to work or be conscripted.

24   Greatest escape of the war: twenty-nine officers tunnel out of Holzminden PoW camp. In America four lightless nights a week are ordered.

26   Sugar ration in America reduced to 2lbs per person a month.

29　Munitions workers' strike ends.

30　Sir Charles Fielding appointed as Director General of Food Production. British coal production at lowest war level, due to influenza.

August

1　Mr Balfour makes a speech about the League of Nations. RFP now at 118 per cent. In France the Chamber votes for the 1920 class to be called up. In Germany the 1920 class is already at the field depots but, for political reasons, not in the field.

3　British ambulance transport *Warilda* sunk in the Channel with the loss of 125 lives. Cuba announces conscription for men aged 21 to 28.

4　Riots and unrest across Japan over high rice prices. Bishop of London consecrates war shrine in Hyde Park.

5　Final Zeppelin raid. All bombs dropped in the sea and one brought down 40 miles from land. Lloyd George tells the British Empire to 'Hold fast'. In America the number of pages in a newspaper reduced to save paper. Ex-Interior Minister Valpy found guilty and sentenced to five years exile.

8　Education Act receives Royal Assent; raises school-leaving age to 14.

9　Executive of Miners' Federation appeals to miners to increase output of coal by avoiding unnecessary absenteeism. Italian aircraft drop leaflets on Vienna calling on them to throw off Prussian servitude.

10　United States Coast Guard station and lighthouse on Smith Island, North Carolina, attacked by gas from U-boat.

11　German air raid on Calais causes sixty casualties.

12　The sale of liquor is banned on American railways.

13　First women recruited into the US Marine Corps.

17　Japanese government releases all rice stocks for sale at a fair price. In Britain, 11,000 bus and tram workers strike and secure a 5s. weekly rise for women.

21　Reichstag party leaders informed of peace efforts.

22　Over a million people sign a petition demanding the internment of all aliens. Rally in Hyde Park about aliens and their internment.

25　A three-day tube strike secures equal pay. In Berlin rioters smash pictures of the Kaiser. In Hungary the government expels Jews and confiscates their property.

30　London Police strike. The strikers demand an increased war bonus, reinstatement of a dismissed constable and official recognition of the Police Union. Austrians notify Berlin of their intention to take independent peace action.

31　London Police strike settled; the men return to work. Over 700,000 working days lost during the month.

September

1 RFP 116 per cent.
3 Civilian populations of Cambrai and Douai evacuated by the Germans to Belgium.
4 A shortage of coal forces closure of Italian munitions plants.
5 Arrest in London of M. Litvinov and other Bolsheviks as guarantees for the safety of British subjects in Russia. Berlin and Brandenburg are declared to be in a state of siege.
6 Aircraft workers in Manchester strike.
10 The Kaiser receives no response after addressing 1,500 Krupp workers.
13 Railway strike begins in South Wales.
15 Final air raid on Paris causes thirty-seven casualties.
20 RAF bomb and drop leaflets on Constantinople.
22 Price of meat rises by 2*d.*/lb.
24 Railway strike, which had begun in South Wales, spreads to other lines, affecting the GWR, Midland and the London and South Western.
26 Railway strike in England ended. Bulgaria requests an armistice.
27 Bulgaria proclaimed a republic.
30 The Chancellor of the Exchequer opens a 'Feed the Guns' campaign to raise a second War Loan of £1,000,000,000.

October

1 Wages (Men and Women) Committee begins. RFP now 129 per cent; the increase is caused by price rises in butter, eggs, meat and milk. The influenza pandemic in America shuts some war plants.
3 Tsar Ferdinand of Bulgaria abdicates.
4 Explosion in a shell-loading factory in New Jersey kills ninety.
8 Food Controller takes over milk distribution and jam to be rationed. British bomb Metz.
11 Canada forbids strikes and lockouts.
12 Germany accepts Wilson conditions.
13 Portuguese government crushes a military uprising in Coimbra, Lisbon and Oporto.
14 The King presents £10,000 to the Red Cross; Prince of Wales donates £3,000. General strike in Bohemia (Austria).
16 Brazil closes German banks. Peace demonstrations in Berlin.
17 London subscribes £31 million in National War Bonds in nine days.
18 British bomb Constantinople.
21 British planes raid Frankfurt in daylight.

23	British bombers attack Kaiserslautern and Wiesbaden.
26	Stonehenge given to the nation. In Berlin, Ludendorff resigns.
27	Austria and Germany ask for an armistice.
31	Serious influenza epidemic in London; 2,200 deaths in the last week. In Vienna workers and students demonstrate against the Hapsburgs. British air raid on Bonn kills twenty-six, severely wounds thirty-six and slightly wounds a further twenty people. Revolutions in Budapest and Vienna.

November

1	RFP 133 percent.
2	Mass meeting of trade unionists in London to consider Labour's part in the peace. Subway incident in New York kills 97 and injures 100.
3	German Navy mutiny at Kiel. Austrians sign armistice.
4	Garrison troops and workers join the mutiny that spreads to Bremen, Cuxhaven, Hamburg, Lübeck, Travemünde and Wilhelmshaven.
5	General strike in Berlin.
6	Austrian Army formally demobilised.
7	Appointment of Civil Department of Demobilisation and Resettlement. Health Ministry Bill introduced into the Commons. Bavaria declared a republic when king flees to Austria. New York celebrates the armistice after incorrect despatch from United Press.
8	Jam rationing begins.
9	German republic proclaimed.
10	Kaiser crosses into Holland.
11	War ends. In Paris AA guns fire 1,200 shots. From 11 am church bells ring to celebrate the armistice.
13	Crown Prince crosses into Holland. Austrian republic proclaimed.
14	Interned RND sailors sail home.
15	In Britain the meat ration for Christmas is to be doubled.
16	Speech by Lloyd George opens election campaign.
19	British Government announce war casualties – over three million, of which nearly one million dead.
21	President Wilson signs Prohibition Act.
23	League football resumes.
25	Parliament dissolves. Bulk of lighting restrictions lifted.
29	Prisoner of war ship docks at Hull.

December

1   RFP down 4 per cent. Car drivers allowed to travel freely within 30 miles of home. First troops return to America.

4   British Army demobilisation begins.

6   Rail strike in Britain ends with new working day of eight hours.

9   British insurers discontinue war risk insurance. Shop lighting limits removed for Christmas. Pivotal men begin to be released from the forces. Cotton workers win 40 per cent pay rise.

11   All edible offal removed from food rationing in Britain.

12   Men over 41 called up in 1918 to be mobilised.

14   Start of the Khaki/Coupon election. Munitionette volunteers released.

16   Unlimited mileage on car travel allowed.

18   British Information Ministry abolished.

21   British children's sugar allowance increased.

22   All food regulations suspended in America.

25   British Christmas holiday extended to 28th.

28   British General Election results: Tories win 384 seats – now dominant partner of the government coalition.

29   British meat ration coupon value rises from 4d to 5d and game, pork, poultry and preserved meats unrestricted.

31   Annual births lowest of the war at 848,519.

GWI-HF_269 As with photo 236, a card to cash in on popular sentiment.

Victory Greetings

NOW AND FOREVER

Long may they hold their own
'Gainst all invaders,
Soldiers of Foch and Haig,
And Pershing's Crusaders.

GWI-HF_271 Postcard publishers in America were just as quick as those in Britain to see a market for victory cards.

GWI-HF_270 During the war, many streets had a Roll of Honour. Now with the war over, one street, along with photographs of their lost ones, reminded everyone of the overall cost to the nation.

Bibliography, Sources and Further Reading

British Food Policy during the First World War. Allen & Unwin. 1985.

Becker, J. *The Great War and the French People*. Berg. 1990.

Bilton, D. *Hull in the Great War*. Pen & Sword. 2015.

Bilton, D. *Reading in the Great War*. Pen & Sword. 2015.

Bilton, D. *The Home Front in the Great War – Aspects of Conflict*. Leo Cooper. 2003.

Charman, I. *The Great War, The People's Story*. Random House. 2014.

Fridenson, P. (Ed.) *The French Home Front. 1914-1918*. Berg. 1992.

Gregory, A. *The Last Great War. British Society and the First World War*. Cambridge University Press. 2008.

Hastings, M. *Catastrophe*. William Collins. 2013.

Herwig, H.H. *The First World War. Germany and Austria-Hungary 1914-1918*. Arnold. 1997.

Horn, P. *Rural Life in England in the First World War*. Gill and MacMillan. 1984.

Kennedy, R. *The Children's War*. Palgrave Macmillan. 2014.

Kocka, J. *Facing Total War. German Society 1914-1918*. Berg. 1984.

Markham, J. *Keep the Home Fires Burning*. Highgate Publications. 1988.

Martin, C. *English Life in the First World War*. Wayland. 1974.

Marwick, A. *The Deluge. British Society and the First World War*. Macmillan. 1973.

Marwick, A. *Women at War*. Fontana. 1977.

McGrandle, L. *The Cost of Living in Britain*. Wayland. 1974.

Philpott, Wing Commander I., *The Birth of the Royal Air Force*. Pen & Sword. 2013.

The Berkshire Chronicle.

The Hull Times.

The Hull Daily Mail.

The Reading Standard.

Turner, E.S. *Dear Old Blighty*. Michael Joseph. 1980.

Unknown. *History of the War*. Volumes 16 to 21. The Times. 1918 to 1920.

Unknown. *The Illustrated War News*. Illustrated London News and Sketch, Ltd., 1918.

Unknown. *Illustrated London News*. January–December 1918. Illustrated London News and Sketch Ltd., 1918.

Williams, J. *The Home Fronts*. Constable & Co Ltd. 1972.

Winter, J. M. *The Experience of World War I*. Equinox (Oxford) Ltd. 1986.

Wilson, H.W. (Ed.) *The Great War. The Standard History of the All Europe Conflict*. Volumes 11 and 12. Amalgamated Press 1919.

INDEX